Hansel and Gretel

ISBN 0 573 16402 9

Please see page iv for further copyright information

CHARACTERS

The Forest Fairy
Attrocia the Witch
Karl, a young forester
Dame Do-Good
Sir Rupert de Rottweiler, Mayor of Pumpernickel
Lucy Lockett, the Mayor's kitchen-maid
Hansel } the Dame's grandchildren
Gretel }
Potz } the Mayor's bailiffs
Panz }
Dickie Dymwit, the Dame's beau
Melindra, the Gypsy Queen
Roderigo, a gypsy

Chorus of **Villagers, Fairies, Gingerbread Men, Mice, Servants, Gypsies,** etc.

SYNOPSIS OF SCENES

ACT I

Prologue	The Realm of the Forest Fairy
Scene 1	The Village of Pumpernickel
Scene 2	A Quiet Street
Scene 3	The Village Fête at Siezitt Hall
Scene 4	The Edge of the Great Forest
Scene 5	A Clearing in the Forest

ACT II

Scene 6	Back at the Village
Scene 7	A Path in the Forest
Scene 8	Outside the Gingerbread House
Scene 9	Behind the Gingerbread House
Scene 10	The Witch's Kitchen
Scene 11	A Corridor in the Town Hall
Scene 12	The Mayor's Parlour and Finale

MUSICAL NUMBERS

ACT I

1	**Song/Dance**	Villagers
1a	**Song/Dance** (Reprise)	Karl and Villagers
2	**Song**	Lucy
3	**Song**	Dickie
4	**Song**	Karl
5	**Song**	Lucy
6	**Song/Dance**	Villagers and Guests
7	**Song**	Potz and Panz
8	**Song**	Dickie and Dame
9	**Song/Dance**	Gypsies
10	**Music**	Company

ACT II

11	**Song**	Villagers
12	**Song**	Karl
13	**Song**	Sir Rupert, Potz and Panz
14	**Dance**	Gingerbread Men
15	**Song**	Karl and Lucy
16	**Song**	Dame, Potz, Panz, Dickie
17	**Song**	Hansel and Gretel
18	**Song**	Company
19	**Song**	Dickie and Audience

SONG SUGGESTIONS

For Norman Robbins' list of song suggestions, please contact the Librarian, c/o Samuel French Ltd, 52 Fitzroy Street, London W1T 5JR.

AUTHOR'S NOTES AND PRODUCTION HINTS

Though one of the best known tales of brothers Jakob and Wilhelm Grimm for almost a hundred years, theatrical versions of *Hansel and Gretel* have been children's *plays* and seldom, if ever, presented as "traditional" pantomimes. Why this should be is not quite clear, for the story contains almost all the elements required for successful adaptation. A strong story, a wicked witch, and good triumphing over what, at first, would appear to be a terrible occurrence. Perhaps the fault lay with the fact that only five characters appear in the original story? Hansel and Gretel, their ill-matched parents and the terrible witch. Composer Engelbert Humperdinck (1854–1921) expanded the cast in his 1893 operatic version with the character of The Sandman (who lulls the lost children to sleep, but fulfils no other purpose). Recently seeing the opera again, and remembering the play version I saw at the Guthrie Theatre in Minneapolis during the winter of 1979, I once again began wondering why no pantomime version was available and decided to write one myself to see if it would work. The result is this version of what I regard as a wrongly neglected masterpiece.

My only concession to the modern-day curse of political correctness is to request that the character of the witch, no matter how blood-curdling her utterances are, should be played extremely tongue-in-cheek. She is, in fact, far less evil than she imagines herself to be and is a classic case of someone who confidently shoots herself in the foot every time she opens her mouth. If one recollects the appalling Mad Madame Mimm from the Disney cartoon film *The Sword in the Stone*, you'll have the character to perfection.

In the kitchen scene of Act II, I have indicated a method of mopping up the mess as the scene proceeds, but if you don't want to use the witch's broom, keep an off-stage mop to hand, which Dickie can use at will. It is useful to have a member of the stage crew under the counter to help with other effects, and if space is at a premium (and in some small halls it may be) when the chorus enter, they can be used to move the counter further upstage just before the song begins.

Apart from that, have fun.

Norman Robbins 2005

To the memory of
John Rich
and
Edward Leman Blanchard
who made it all possible

Other pantomimes by Norman Robbins
published by Samuel French Ltd

Aladdin
Ali Baba and the Forty Thieves
Babes in the Wood
Cinderella
Dick Whittington
The Grand Old Duke of York
Hickory Dickory Dock
Humpty Dumpty
Jack and the Beanstalk
Jack and Jill
The Old Woman Who Lived in a Shoe
Puss in Boots
Red Riding Hood
Rumpelstiltzkin
Sing a Song of Sixpence
The Sleeping Beauty
Snow White
Tom, the Piper's Son
The Wonderful Story of Mother Goose
The White Cat

Plays by Norman Robbins
published by Samuel French Ltd

The Late Mrs Early
Nightmare
Pull the Other One
Slaughterhouse
Tiptoe Through the Tombstones
Tomb with a View
Wedding of the Year

ACT I

Prologue

The Realm of the Forest Fairy

The CURTAIN *rises to reveal a lane backdrop depicting an idyllic forest setting of trees, waterfall and stream, etc., with dappled lighting*

Melodious strains of music play

The Forest Fairy, carrying a wand, enters in a white follow-spot and strikes an attitude

Fairy Thrice welcome to my forest realm; a place as old as Time.
Where our intent's to charm you with a brand new pantomime.
It starts in Pumpernickel Village, (quaint and rather small)
Which stands beside a gurgling stream and dancing waterfall.
No noisy traffic fills the streets; its air is sweet and pure,
And sorrow's not permitted there. Of that you may be sure.
In short, a more idyllic spot you'll very seldom find,
For all who dwell there live in bliss and hearts are true and kind.

Attrocia the Witch enters L *in a green follow-spot. She is very myopic and wears a pair of bottle-bottom spectacles*

Attrocia How absolutely boring. Why, their life's just one big yawn.
It's plain to see it's up to me to make them rue the day they're born.
With evil spells and wicked deeds, an end I'll bring to peace.
Before your tale concludes, I vow, all happiness shall cease. (*She laughs*)
Fairy (*sighing*) Oh, dear. It's old Attrocia. I knew she'd show her face.
(*To her*) Do go away. Or once again, I'll have to put you in your place.
I thought, by now, you'd realize your plans I'll always foil.
Success shall never crown your head, no matter how you toil
Attrocia That could have been so, long ago, but times have changed, my friend
No longer fairies rule the roost. Your reign is at an end
With ev'ry passing day, you'll find I've gained the upper hand,
And malice, spite and discontent will freely spread across this land.
Fairy As usual, you count your chicks some time before they're hatched.
You'll find, 'gainst me, your so-called pow'rs are sadly undermatched.
Despite your threats, without a doubt, you're heading for a fall;
For in this realm I still protect the lives of one and all.

Attrocia (*smirking*) So be it, then, deluded sprite. Our contest we'll begin.
From this hour on, our battle starts. And let the best one win. (*She cackles*)

Attrocia exits L

The follow-spot is extinguished

Fairy (*to the audience*) Fear not. Whatever nasty scheme Attrocia has in mind,
It won't succeed. I'll see to that — as once again she'll find.
(*Smiling*) But time is passing and our story hasn't yet begun.
So come. To Pumpernickel. And rejoice in village fun.

The Fairy waves her wand and exits R

The follow-spot is extinguished

Scene 1

The Village of Pumpernickel

The lane backdrop opens to reveal, in the foreground, quaint cottages and shops suggesting a Germanic fifteenth-century setting, with, behind them, a backdrop depicting a thick pine forest. The Dame's cottage is DR, *and has a practical door*

When the scene begins, it is a bright, sunny morning and the Villagers are singing and dancing

Song and Dance 1 (*Villagers*)

At the end of the song, Karl, a young forester, enters UR, *and moves* DC. *A longbow and quiver of arrows hang at his back*

The Villagers fall back

Karl (*lightly*) The same old Pumpernickel. Everyone enjoying themselves and nobody working. (*Plaintively*) Why can't *I* live here?

1st Villager (*amused*) You could. If you married Lucy Lockett. Everyone knows she's madly in love with you.

All agree

Karl (*surprised*) The Mayor's kitchen-maid?

2nd Villager (*indignantly*) There's nothing wrong with being a kitchen-maid.

Karl (*hastily*) Well, of course there isn't. She's the most beautiful girl I've ever seen. But how on earth could she love me? A poor forester with hardly a penny to his name.

Old Woman It's nothing to do with money, young Karl. When I agreed to marry my young man, everyone thought it was because he'd been left a fortune by his father. But it wasn't.

Old Man No. She'd have married him no matter who'd left him the fortune.

The Old Woman reacts. Everyone laughs

Karl (*brightly*) Well, I'm sure there's no-one who'll leave me a fortune. I haven't a relative in the world. But as long as I have my bow and arrows, there's not a happier man alive. So come. Give me another verse of that song you were singing a moment ago and I'll carry it in my heart for the rest of the day.

Song and Dance 1a (*Karl and Villagers*) Reprise

They all exit variously

A moment later Dame Do-Good bustles in UR. *She is a lady of uncertain age, dressed in an outrageous outfit designed by the local charity shop. She moves* DC, *face wreathed in smiles*

Dame Oh, I say ... Nobody told me we'd started. I've been standing over there (*indicating off* R) talking to the Stage Manager. (*Awed*) And what a state he's in. (*She grimaces*) Talk about black eyes. I've never seen anything like 'em. "Good Heavens," I said, "what happened to you?" "Well," he said, "I was in church last Sunday and when we got up to sing the first hymn, I noticed the woman in front of me had her dress caught up in the cheeks of her bottom." (*To an audience member, reprovingly*) There's no need to look shocked, dear. It's happened to all of us. (*To others*) Hasn't it, girls? (*Continuing with her story*) "Anyway," he said, "I didn't want her to feel embarrassed, so before anybody else noticed, I leaned over and pulled it out for her. Well — quick as a flash — she turned round and punched me right in the eye." (*To an audience member*) Can you believe it? Giving the feller a black eye for trying to do her a good deed. (*Resuming the story*) "And how did you get the other one?" I said. "Well," he said, "half an hour later we stood up for the second hymn and I saw it had happened *again*. Now I'm no *fool*", he said, "I'd learned *my* lesson. If that's how she wanted it, it could stay there. But just as we started singing, the little old lady next to me spotted it and she pulled it out. Well," he said, "I was horrified. I didn't want her getting a black eye as well, so I dropped my hymn book, leaned over — and *stuffed it back in again.*" (*Kindly*) Still ... I expect he'll be all right in a few more days. (*Remembering*) Oh. But I'd better introduce meself, hadn't I? Do-Good's the name. Dyspepsia Do-Good. All round Good Sport and Widow of this Parish. (*She drops a curtsy*) Oooh, but it's nice to see new faces in the village. It's ever so quiet, here, you know. Nothing exciting's happened since a burglar broke into the Town Hall last month and pinched all the Council Tax. They hadn't a clue who'd done it at first because he hadn't left any fingerprints, but he'd made a mistake, you see, this burglar. He'd dropped his *gloves* on the floor. Lovely soft *leather* ones. And the next day they had all the DNA they wanted. Two weeks later they arrested a cow in Scotland. (*She chortles*) Do you like cows? I do. Especially the two down the road. Buttercup and Daisy. (*Proudly*) The only cows in the world that can actually talk. Oh, yes. I was having a chat with them this morning when suddenly Old Farmer Giles opened the gate and shoved a great big bull into the field. There he stood — shaking his horns, foaming at the mouth and pawing at the ground — and poor Buttercup nearly fainted. "Oh, Daisy," she said. "Do you think he's going to charge us?" "I certainly hope not," said Daisy, "I've only got fifty p." (*Remembering*) Here — and talking about money, I need a few pounds myself, so I'd better be off. The Mayor put an advert in the (*local paper*) last week: "Cook wanted for Town Hall", so I applied for the job and I'm on my way there to find out if I've got it. (*Glancing off* L) Ooooh, and here he comes now. The Mayor himself. Sir Rupert de Rottweiler. (*She hastily tidies herself up*)

Sir Rupert de Rottweiler, Mayor of Pumpernickel, enters UL. *He is a self-important personage and disliked by everyone*

Sir Rupert Aha. (*Moving* DC, *sneering*) Dame Do-Good. Just the woman I'm looking for.

Dame (*excitedly*) Oooh. I say. Have I got it, then?

Sir Rupert (*blankly*) Got it?

Dame The Town Hall cook's job.

Sir Rupert (*scornfully*) Certainly not. I wouldn't let you cook at the Town Hall if the councillors were starving.

Dame I don't see why not. I've got recipes Gordon Ramsay (*or other top chef*)'s never even heard of.

Sir Rupert Such as, for instance?

Dame Well ... (*She thinks*) Liver and Soap-flakes casserole.

Sir Rupert (*incredulously*) Liver and Soap-flakes casserole? It must taste horrible.

Dame Yes. But the plates come up lovely and clean when you wash 'em.

Sir Rupert Bah. You know nothing about cooking, you moth-eaten old harridan.

Dame (*indignantly*) I beg your puddin'. (*Proudly*) I once cooked dinner for (*Prime Minister*) and all his Cabinet members in the Houses of Parliament.

Sir Rupert (*startled*) Really?

Dame Yes. (*Prime Minister*) wanted a well-cooked steak with a teensy-weensy sliver of Camembert cheese on top.

Sir Rupert And what about his vegetables?

Dame (*disgustedly*) Oh, *them.* They just had egg and chips.

Sir Rupert Bah. I don't believe a word of it. (*With menace*) But what I do believe is that you've been taking in lodgers without my permission.

Dame (*blankly*) Lodgers?

Sir Rupert Yes. Two snivelling little brats named Hansel and Gretel. (*He glares at the Dame*)

Dame (*chuckling*) Silly old sausage. (*She pushes him playfully*) Hansel and Gretel aren't lodgers. They're little children. I'm just looking after them for a few days while their mum and dad find somewhere else to live. (*Beaming*) They sold their old house in (*local area*) last week for half a million pounds.

Sir Rupert (*impressed*) Did they, indeed?

Dame Mind you'... Their landlord'll go crackers when he finds out. (*She chortles*)

Sir Rupert (*after a reaction*) Yes. Well he won't be the only miserable one if you don't hand over the rent you owe. You'll be looking for a new house yourself.

Dame (*startled*) Eh?

Sir Rupert You haven't paid a penny for the past ten years, so cough it up now or you and your precious Hansel and Gretel will be out the street tonight. (*He holds out his hand for the rent*)

Dame (*in disbelief*) You can't throw *me* out. I've got squatter's rights.

Sir Rupert Looks more like rickets, to me. (*Firmly*) Well — make up your mind. Either pay what you owe, or it's bye-bye to Pumpernickel Village. (*He smirks*)

Dame (*to the audience, unhappily*) What am I going to do? I haven't a penny in the world. (*Suddenly remembering*) Here. I wonder if that feller down the road'll lend it to me? He's got more money than David Beckham. (*Or some other very rich person*)

Sir Rupert (*scornfully*) Don't be ridiculous.

Dame (*protesting*) He has, you know. He's got five private jet-planes, three luxury yachts, six Rolls-Royces and a reserved parking space in (*local car park*) (*Impressed*) And to think ... When he came to this country last month, he was as broke as I am and only knew three words of English.

Sir Rupert (*curiously*) And what were *they?*

Dame Stick 'em up. (*She chortles and pushes him playfully*)

Sir Rupert goes flying, then recovers his balance and storms back to her in annoyance

Sir Rupert Bah. Enough of this badinage. As you obviously can't pay your rent, you'd better start packing at once. I'll have the bailiffs round in fifteen minutes.

Sir Rupert exits huffily DL

Dame (*stricken*) Oh, I say — I'm going to be depicted. And I've lived in that cottage ever since I was a teenager. Nearly twelve years. (*Brightening*) Mind you ... I don't think the roof's going to last much longer. I found death-watch beetles in the attic this morning. All wearing safety helmets. (*Her face crumples*) But I am going to miss it. (*She begins to sob*)

Lucy Lockett enters UR. *She is a very pretty girl in Bavarian-style servant costume, carrying a small basket covered by a cloth*

Lucy (*seeing the Dame*) Dame Do-Good. (*She hurries down to her in concern*) Whatever's the matter?

Dame (*sniffling*) Oh, Lucy. It's that nasty old boss of yours. He's turning me into the street 'cos I can't pay the rent. (*She sobs*)

Lucy (*dismayed*) Oh, no. He can't be that cruel. (*Firmly*) Let me have a word with him. Ask him to let you stay.

Dame (*dabbing at her eyes*) I wish you could. (*Helpfully*) I'd even make a deal with him. If he'll forget half the rent, I'll forget the other half.

Lucy (*amused*) He wouldn't do that, I'm afraid. (*Encouragingly*) But if you paid him something, I'm sure he'd change his mind.

Dame (*protesting*) But I haven't got anything. Not even food for tonight's dinner. I'm flat busted. (*She stops and glares at someone in the audience before continuing*) Even when I was little, our family were the poorest in the village. Whenever the Tooth Fairy came round, she had to leave IOUs.

Lucy (*firmly*) Then you take this basket of groceries (*she gives the basket to the Dame*) and I'll see if the other villagers can spare a few coins. They'd never see you homeless — especially now you're looking after Hansel and Gretel.

Dame (*overcome*) Oh, I say ...

Lucy So cheer up. It'll all be sorted out before you can say Jack Robinson.

Song 2 (*Lucy*)

At the end of the song, the Dame exits into her cottage R *and Lucy exits* DL. *As they do so, Hansel and Gretel enter* UL. *They are nine years old or so, dressed in Austrian-style costume. Hansel carries a small plastic pail*

Hansel (*impatiently*) Hurry up, Gretel. It's nearly lunchtime. (*Moving* DC, *happily*) Just think how pleased she's going to be when she sees what we've picked. (*Displaying the pail*) A whole pail-full of blackberries.

Gretel (*following him* DC) You mean, half a pail-full. You've eaten more than we've got left.

Hansel (*indignantly*) I didn't do it by myself, you know. You've had just as many as me. And took the biggest ones.

Gretel (*defensively*) Well, I got scratched the most, didn't I? (*Dreamily*) But oh, Hansel, didn't they taste wonderful?

Hansel (*happily*) And there's plenty more where these came from.

Gretel But best of all — we didn't have to break our promise to Aunt Dyspepsia.

Hansel (*puzzled*) What promise?

Gretel That we wouldn't go into the forest on our own, silly. In case we got lost.

Hansel Oh, that. (*Scornfully*) But we didn't mean it, did we? We couldn't get lost in that stupid old forest.

Gretel (*uncertainly*) It is rather big.

Hansel But there's plenty of paths. And if we stuck to those, we could easily find our way back.

Gretel There might be wild animals.

Hansel And there might be bigger and better blackberry bushes.

Gretel (*weakening*) Oh, Hansel. I do love blackberries.

Hansel So do I. And when I'm grown up, I'm going to eat them every single day.

Gretel When I'm grown up, I'm going to eat them *twice* a day.

They giggle with delight

(*Eagerly*) Shall we have just another one each?

Hansel (*glancing into the pail*) Better not. I think we've eaten more than we thought. I can see the bottom of the pail.

Gretel (*gazing into the pail; dismayed*) Hardly any left at all.

Hansel (*disappointedly*) Well, we can't take these to Aunt Dyspepsia. There aren't even enough to make a pie. And she's sure to ask us where we've been.

Gretel (*thinking quickly*) I know. We'll pretend we've been down at the duck-pond. Then as soon as it's safe, we'll sneak out again and gather some more.

Hansel Good idea. We'll have blackberry pie for *supper.*

They giggle and exit into the cottage. As the door closes, Dickie Dimwit enters UR, *and moves* DC. *He is a zany character, eternally cheerful, though not over-blessed with intelligence*

Dickie (*beaming*) Hiya, kids.

Audience response

(*Pulling a face*) Is that the best you can do? (*Mockingly*) Hiya. (*Firmly*) Now come on. It's pantomime, this is. When I shout "Hiya, kids", you're supposed to shout back at the top of your voices. Not whisper (*mockingly*) "Hiya." It's not like the vicar's tea-party, you know. (*Imitating a toothy, stereotypical theatrical vicar*) "Hallo, children". (*Firmly*) This is all-out war. (*He snarls savagely*) I want you to shout and scream and yell. Bring the roof down. Pretend you're in Tesco's (*or other major supermarket*) and your mother won't buy you a pack of your favourite food — Brussel Sprouts. (*He grimaces*) And all you mums and dads and grannies and grandads — don't think you can wriggle out of it. Oh, no. I want you to make twice as much noise. So come on, fellers — undo your top buttons and loosen your belts — and all the ladies (*he hesitates*) — well, you make your own arrangements. (*Briskly*) Right. We'll have another go. I'm going to go off and come on again, and when I do, I'm going to shout "Hiya, kids" and I want you all to shout back "Hiya, Dickie" as loud as you possibly can. (*Threateningly*) And if anybody doesn't shout — I'm going to ask the lighting feller to put a spotlight on you, so everybody can see what a rotten old spoilsport you are. (*He grins*) Right. I'm going off now.

Dickie exits quickly L, *then enters at once*

Hiya, kids.

Audience response

(*Covering his ears; pained*) I didn't say you had to deafen me. (*He chuckles*) Still — now we've got the *daft* bit out of the way, we can get down to the serious stuff. (*Seriously*) Well — it's not all laughs, you know. Not round here. You wouldn't believe the problems some folks have. The feller next door to me, for instance. He got a new job last week. As a glass blower. He'd only been at it ten minutes, when he forgot what he was doing and instead of blowing out, he sucked in. (*He grimaces*) They had to send him home later with a pane in his stomach. And then there's the chap in (*local street*) who tried to make a living by opening a shop and got sent to *jail*. (*Amazed*) Can you believe it? Sent to jail for opening a shop. (*Musing*) Mind you — it was half-past twelve at night and it wasn't his own shop. (*Grinning*) But me. Well ... (*Regretfully*) I haven't got a job.

Audience response

No, no. Don't be sorry for me. I've not had a job since I came out of the navy. (*Grinning*) Ahhhh ... you didn't know I'd been a sailor, did you? Well, I was. (*Wryly*) But I had to pack it in 'cos one day the captain shouted "All hands on deck" and some fool trod on my fingers. (*Happily*) But it's great, not having to work 'cos I can spend all me time trying to make folks laugh. 'Cos that's what life's about, isn't it, kids? Having a laugh. And if I had my way, that's what everybody in the world would be doing right this very minute. (*Enthusiastically*) Being happy.

Song 3 (*Dickie*)

As he sings, Villagers may enter and join in. At the end of the song, all exit variously. As they do so, the Lights dim and Attrocia enters DL

Attrocia (*sneering*) For happiness you'll dream in vain,
O mortal of restricted brain.
Your village, from this very hour,
Shall tremble 'neath my awesome power.
This Green (*she indicates it*) — reserved for your carousing
Soon will boast new council housing ...
Plus, of course, a special treat ...
(*Nastily*) A mobile phone-mast on each street.
On yonder hill (*she indicates off*) where children play,
A wind-farm, shrieking night and day.
And here's a thought to freeze your blood ...
(*Triumphantly*) All public toilets closed for good. (*She cackles in delight*)

The Fairy enters R *in a white spot*

Fairy (*amused*) Oh, dear. Oh, dear. Those wicked schemes,
For you, will stay no more than dreams
The spell I've cast upon this place
Will banish evil, without trace.
No matter where, round here, you lurk.
Your magic simply will not work.

Attrocia (*snarling*) You think not? Then try this for size.
(*Casting a spell*) Come hail and lightning from the skies.
River flood. Destroy the bridge.

Nothing happens

(*Dismayed*) Saints preserve us. Not a sossidge.
Fairy Satisfied? I've proved my point.
Your nose is truly out of joint.
No reason have you now to stay,
So fare-thee-well, my friend. (*Brightly*) Good-day.

The Fairy exits R

Attrocia (*fuming*) Ten thousand curses. Foiled again.
That fairy's gone too far.
If magic will not help me *here*
I'll have to use it from afar …
But rest assured, I'll win the day,
And that I guarantee.
The victor's crown, before tonight,
Will find its way to me.
(*She cackles with glee*)

Attrocia exits L

The Lights return to normal

Potz and Panz enter UR. *They are local layabouts, not too bright, and both wearing ill-fitting bailiff uniforms with battered felt hats*

Potz (*ambling* DC, *beaming*) Oooh, isn't it exciting, Panz? Our first day as Town Bailiffs.
Panz (*following*) Yes. But it's a good job we didn't get the job yesterday.
Potz (*blankly*) Why's that?
Panz I had to go to a funeral, didn't I? (*He removes his hat and clutches it to his heart*) Me poor old Uncle Harry died. From deafness.
Potz (*sneering*) Don't be stupid. How could he die from deafness?
Panz He didn't hear the steamroller coming. (*He replaces his hat*)
Potz (*after a reaction*) Now listen. If we're going to impress Sir Rupert and keep these jobs for good, we've got to get rid of Dame Do-Good and those cheeky kids she's looking after. (*Indignantly*) I caught 'em this morning making everybody laugh by pretending to be us.
Panz (*affronted*) I hope you said something to 'em.

Potz (*proudly*) I certainly did. I told 'em to stop acting like idiots.
Panz (*unhappily*) My *brother's* an idiot.
Potz (*startled*) Eh?
Panz (*nodding*) Been barmy for years. He thinks he's a dustbin.
Potz And can't the doctor cure him?
Panz I suppose so. But my dad won't let him try.
Potz (*amazed*) Why not?
Panz We'd have nowhere to put the rubbish.

Potz snatches off his hat and beats Panz around the shoulder with it

Oww.
Potz (*glowering*) If brains were gunpowder, you wouldn't have enough to blow your hat off. (*He replaces his hat*) Now stop messing about and let's decide how we're going to do it.
Panz Do what?
Potz (*exasperated*) Get rid of Dame Do-Good. We've got to get her out of that cottage (*he indicates it*) before Sir Rupert arrives. We don't want to get the sack before we've started, do we?
Panz (*unconcerned*) Doesn't bother me. I'm only doing this till it's time for me to go on television.
Potz (*startled*) Television? You? Doing what?
Panz A new talent show. With half a million pounds as first prize. (*Proudly*) I'm going to do Farmyard Impressions.(*He smirks*)
Potz (*scornfully*) Don't be ridiculous. You'll never win half a million pounds by doing animal noises.
Panz I won't be doing animal noises. I'll be doing the smells.

Potz reacts

Sir Rupert enters DL

Sir Rupert (*sourly*) Well? Have you done what I told you to? Has the old faggot gone?
Potz (*grovelling*) Not yet, Your Wash-up, but leave it to us. We'll have her out of there in two seconds flat. (*To Panz, hastily*) Quick. Knock on the door.

Potz and Panz hurry to the door and stand one to each side of it. Panz mimes knocking and the sound of a very loud Westminster chime is heard. All react

The door opens and Dame Do-Good appears

Dame (*dismayed*) Oh, no. It's Simon Cowell (*or other unpopular personality*) again. He's come to throw me out. And just as I've been mentioned in a brand new book.
Sir Rupert (*surprised*) What book's that?
Dame The telephone directory.
Sir Rupert (*firmly*) Into the street with her.

The Dame wails as Potz and Panz grab her and hurry her DC

The Villagers hurry in UR *and* UL. *An anxious Hansel and Gretel appear in the doorway*

Villagers (*variously*) What's happening? What's wrong? (*Etc.*)
Sir Rupert (*grandly*) By the power invested in me as Mayor of Pumpernickel, I'm turning this flannel-faced old fanfaron out of her cottage for non-payment of rent. (*He smirks*)
Villagers (*variously*) Shame. Boo. Down with Rottweiler. (*Etc.*)
Sir Rupert (*snarling*) Silence, you pathetic pack of petulant peasantry. Another word and I'll have you thrown out, as well.

Lucy enters hastily, DL. *She carries a bag of coins*

Lucy (*breathlessly*) Wait, Sir Rupert. Wait. There's no need to turn her out. Look. (*She shows the bag to Sir Rupert*) I've collected enough money to pay everything she owes. Ninety pounds. (*She holds the money out to him*)

The Villagers cheer. The Dame looks relieved

Sir Rupert (*aside*) Curses. (*Brightening*) But there's still ten pounds owing for Council Tax. Unless she pays that, my pretty little kitchenmaid, *you*'ve been wasting your time. (*He smirks*)

Everyone looks dismayed

Lucy (*aghast*) But it's every penny the villagers can spare.

Karl enters DL

Karl Not quite.

Everyone turns to him in surprise

(*Moving* C) No-one asked me to help out.

Sir Rupert (*annoyed*) Bah. It's that interfering forester, Karl. (*Sharply*) You keep out of this. You don't even live in the village.

Karl (*cheerfully*) That's quite true, Sir Rupert. But it doesn't stop me helping a lady in distress. (*He offers his money pouch*) You'll find the last ten pounds she owes in there.

The Villagers look delighted

Sir Rupert Bah. (*He snatches the pouch in annoyance*) You haven't heard the last of this, forester. No-one gets away with making *me* look a fool. (*To Potz and Panz*) Come along, you bungling bailiffs. Back to the Town Hall.

Sir Rupert storms off L, *followed by the sheepish-looking bailiffs*

The Villagers laugh delightedly

Hansel and Gretel run to the Dame and hug her

Lucy (*to Karl*) I'm afraid you've made a very bad enemy.

Karl I wouldn't be surprised. But hopefully I've also made a few new friends.

Dame (*beaming*) Well you're certainly a friend of *mine*.

Hansel
Gretel } (*together*) *And* ours.

Dame And I know just the way to thank you for what you've done for me, today. Why don't you come inside and have a nice bit of lunch? I can do you one of my world famous "five-second" boiled eggs.

Karl (*surprised*) Five-second boiled eggs? Surely they need boiling for longer than that?

Dame I know. But if I hold them in the water any longer, I scald my fingers.

Karl (*amused*) It's very kind of you, Dame Do-Good, but I really don't need any thanks. I'm just happy I was able to help.

Lucy But you've given away all your money. How will you manage now?

Karl Who needs money when friends surround you? There's a thousand ways of cheering yourself up when things start looking gloomy, but I know the very best of them all.

Lucy And what's that?

Song 4 (*Karl*)

As the song progresses, the others join in singing and dancing

At the end of the song, the Lights fade to Black-out

Scene 2

A Quiet Street

A lane scene with full lighting

Dickie enters R *carrying a large, white-painted notice-board, its face away from the audience. On it is written, in large black letters, "Do not press this button". Below the words is a large red button, about one inch thick. A hanging wire, or a hook, is fixed to its back making it possible to display it on a wall*

Dickie (*to the audience*) Hiya, kids.

Audience response

Here — you'll never guess what I've found. This funny old notice-board. (*He shows it to the audience*) And look what it says. (*He turns it round so they can read it*) "Do *not* press this button." (*Puzzled*) I wonder what it means? Well — I know what it *means*, but I don't know if it means what I *think* it means. I mean it *might* mean what I *think* it means, or it might mean it means something I *don't* know it means — if you see what I mean? (*He thinks*) Do you think I should press it and find out?

Audience response

Are you sure?

Audience response

Oooh, I don't know. Something horrible might happen. (*Brightening*) Mind you — it might be the button that starts the Lotto machine, mightn't it? And (*current Lottery presenter*) might be looking for it. (*Fretting*) But I can't carry it round all day. It doesn't half make your arms ache. (*Brightening*) I know. (*He moves* L) I'll hang it on the wall over here where it'll be safe. (*He hangs the notice-board on the proscenium arch*) Then if anybody does come looking for it, I'll know where it is and collect the reward. 'Cos there's bound to be a reward, isn't there? (*Worried*) Mind you — if there is a reward, and anybody else knows about it, then they could claim it instead of me and I wouldn't get anything. (*He thinks*) So I'll tell you what we'll do. If you see anybody trying to touch it, can you all shout "Dickie" at the top of your voices and wherever I am, I'll come rushing back to stop 'em. Will you do that for me? Will you?

Audience response

Oh, smashing.

Hansel and Gretel enter R, *carrying their pail*

Hansel Hallo, Dickie.

Dickie (*beaming*) Hallo, you two. And where are you going?

Gretel To pick more blackberries for Aunt Dyspepsia.

Dickie Oooh. Can I help? I just love blackberries.

Hansel We'd rather do it ourselves, if you don't mind. It's to thank her for taking good care of us.

Gretel But you could keep her busy while we do it. She might be upset if she knew we were in the forest.

Dickie (*startled*) Forest? (*Alarmed*) Ooooooh, you mustn't go in the forest on your own, kids. Not that one. It's ever so dark and gloomy. You might not find your way back.

Hansel Yes, we will. (*He chuckles*) Sir Rupert's going to help us.

Dickie Eh?

Hansel You know those shiny new pebbles he has in his driveway? We're going to fill this pail with them and leave a trail everywhere we go. That way we'll never get lost.

Dickie (*impressed*) Well, you crafty little things. I'd never have thought of that. The first time I went in the forest on my own, I cried my eyes out because my brother had lost his shoes and socks.

Gretel (*puzzled*) But why did that make *you* cry?

Dickie 'Cause I was the one *wearing* 'em.

Hansel (*curious*) So how did you find your way home again?

Dickie I saw a big sign on a tree saying "This way to the Forest Hotel". So, quick as a flash, I got my mobile phone out, sent 'em a text telling 'em to book me a room for the night, then I walked and walked and walked until I finally got there. (*He grimaces*) Trouble is, it was half-past one in the morning and everybody had gone to bed.

Gretel (*wide-eyed*) So you couldn't get in after all?

Dickie No. (*Proudly*) But I wasn't beaten. I just rang the doorbell and banged on a dustbin lid till the landlady woke up and leaned out of her bedroom window to ask me what I wanted. "I'm Dickie Dymwit," I shouted, "and I'm staying here."

Hansel (*relieved*) So she came down to let you in?

Dickie No. She said "Stay there, then", and went back to bed

Gretel (*laughing*) Oh, Dickie. You do make us laugh. But we mustn't stand talking to you all afternoon or we'll never get any berries picked.

Hansel And we've still to collect the pebbles from Sir Rupert's driveway.

Dickie (*concerned*) Well, don't let him see you *doing* it, 'cos he'll be ever so cross if he does. He even shouted at me last week. "Come here, you horrible little monster", he said. "*I'll* teach you to throw stones at my new greenhouse." "I wish you would," I said. "I've missed every time so far." (*He chortles*)

Gretel Don't worry, Dickie. He won't catch us. (*To Hansel*) Come on, Hansel. The sooner we make a start, the better.

Hansel and Gretel exit L

Dickie (*to the audience*) Oh, I do like Hansel and Gretel, don't you? (*He remembers*) But I'd better get going as well, 'cos I'm right in the middle of a fantastic experiment. (*Confidentially*) I'm trying to cross a cement mixer with one of Dame Do-Good's chucky hens. If it works out all right, I should get a *brick*-layer. (*He chortles*) Now don't forget, everybody. If anybody comes near this notice-board, just give me a shout and I'll be right here. See you later.

Dickie exits R. *As he goes, Attrocia enters* L *in a green spot*

Attrocia (*scowling*) By all that's evil, I declare
No matter how I've strived,
That Fairy's ruined all my schemes;
Each nasty plan's nose-dived.
There must be something I can do
To gain the upper hand?
A ruse that's quite sensational,
Magnificently grand ... (*She sniffs the air and glances off* R)
But something wicked comes this way ...
I smell it in the air.
Mayhap 'twill serve to aid my skills?
I'll hide myself o'er there.

Attrocia scuttles off L

The green light vanishes

Sir Rupert enters R, *followed by Potz and Panz*

Sir Rupert Now don't forget. All the important people in the village must be at my stately home, Siezitt Hall, bright and early tomorrow morning. I want to make quite sure they get the best of everything at the village fête before the *commoners* arrive with their hoards of nasty children. How I *hate* them. Whinging and whining little brats, with mobile phones, loud voices and runny noses. Guzzling ice-cream and scoffing everything in sight. If I had my way, they'd never be allowed near respectable people.

Potz (*frowning*) I don't think *that's* very nice. I *like* children, I do.

Panz And *me*. (*Proudly*) There were twenty-seven of us in my family.

Sir Rupert (*gaping at him*) Twenty-seven?

Panz Yes. And everybody's name began with a different letter of the alphabet — except one.

Potz Who was that?

Panz My baby brother. Six and three quarters.

Sir Rupert Six and three quarters?

Panz (*nodding*) Yes. They drew *his* name out of a hat.

Sir Rupert (*disgustedly*) Bah. (*Sharply*) Get over to Siezitt Hall at once and start putting up the tents and loudspeakers.

Sir Rupert crosses L *to the exit*

Potz We can put the tents up, boss, but I don't know about the other stuff

Sir Rupert (*turning back to Potz and Panz with a scowl*) Why not?

Potz (*uneasily*) Well — you know that prize goat of yours? The one that eats everything? Well, he ate the whole sound system, half an hour ago — including the loudspeakers.

Sir Rupert (*aghast*) What? And didn't you rush it to the vet, immediately?

Panz Of course we did. But he told us not to worry. It wouldn't upset it or anything.

Potz We might just get a bit of feedback.

Potz and Panz chortle

Sir Rupert (*scowling*) Bah. Get on with what I told you, and make sure no children start playing around. If there were none in the village at all, the rest of us would be much happier.

Sir Rupert exits

Panz (*looking after him*) Miserable old thing. (*Mocking*) Don't let the children start playing about.

Potz Yes. He's dead mean, he is. But I suppose we'd better get on with it, or he'll be giving us the *sack*. Come on. Let's go find those tents.

Potz and Panz exit R *again. As they do so, Attrocia enters* L, *in a green light*

Attrocia (*thoughtfully*) A village without children.
Now *there's* a happy thought.
Just think what mis'ry that could cause.
If in my net their brats I caught.
But how to tempt 'em? That's the rub
All children know the dangers
Of going where they should not go;
Or taking sweets from strangers.
And yet — and yet — I see a way
To beat that Fairy spell.
Attrocia shall win the day
And rid the world of kids, as well. (*She cackles with glee*)

Attrocia exits L

The green light vanishes

Karl and Lucy enter R

Karl I can't tell you how much I'm looking forward to tomorrow's fête. Everyone in the village is talking about it.

Lucy I'm not surprised. It's the biggest event of the year for them. There'll be dancing round the maypole — all kinds of stalls — a huge barbecue at the edge of the lake and the most wonderful firework display in the evening. (*She sighs*) Not that I'll see much of it. Sir Rupert'll make quite sure his servants are kept busy.

Karl But you're bound to have *some* free time.

Lucy I didn't last year. And besides — he's not too happy with me for trying to stop him from throwing Dame Do-Good out. If he ever discovers I gave her some groceries, too, I don't know what he'll do.

Karl (*amused*) Well — as we both know he's not exactly pleased with me, for the self-same reason, I think we should forget all about him and talk about us. I've only passed through the village before, so perhaps you could show me round while we get to know each other better.

Lucy (*smiling*) What a good idea. So where would you like to start?

Song 5 (*Lucy*)

At the end of the song, the Lights fade rapidly to Black-out

Scene 3

The Village Fête at Siezitt Hall

A full set. The backdrop depicts the magnificent grounds of Siezitt Hall. Masking entrances and exits L *and* R *are ancient trees, clipped hedges and flower borders. Brightly decorated stalls occupy available spaces. The lighting is warm and full*

When the scene begins, guests in their finery are examining the goods on display and stall-holders in peasant-style dress are doing a brisk trade. A balloon seller wanders around selling his/her wares, as do a toffee-apple seller and an ice-cream salesman or woman. Villagers and their children also crowd the area. A group of dancers in bright costumes performs a lively routine as the song progresses

Song and Dance 6 (*Villagers and Guests*)

At the end of the dance, all applaud the dancers who then hurry off. The crowd then drifts off in all directions

Dame Do-Good enters R. *She wears an outrageous new costume and carries a five pound note*

Dame (*moving* C) Oh, I say ... (*She displays the dress*) Do you like it, girls? It's called a "Public Speaking" dress. Long enough to cover the subject, but short enough to be interesting. (*She chortles*) I got it in (*local charity shop*). Yes. They get all sorts of stuff in there, you know. And talk about crowded. You could hardly breathe for bargain hunters. There were six of us at one time trying on the same pair of corsets. And don't you see some odd folks in there? Well, you do in ours. There was one feller thought he was a snooker ball. Every time I looked up, there he was — at the end of a queue. (*Remembering*) Oooh, but I must tell you ... You'll never guess what happened last night. Hansel and Gretel came home with a bucketful of blackberries and I managed to bake two beautiful pies with 'em. We had one for supper and I brought the other one to the fête to sell it. (*Beaming*) And look at what I got for it. (*She displays the five pound note*) A five pound note. If I had a bit more I could buy enough food to last us a week.

Sir Rupert enters R

Sir Rupert (*seeing the Dame and reacting*) Bah ... it's that hideous old harridan, Dame Do-Good. I wonder what she's doing here?

Dame (*turning to see Sir Rupert*) Oooh, I say … The very feller I'm looking for.

Sir Rupert (*taken aback*) I beg your pardon?

Dame Well … *you're* supposed to have more brains than anybody else in the village, aren't you? So it's only fair that you should be first to try it.

Sir Rupert Try what?

Dame The new game that's just come out. I bet you five pounds that you can't say "blackberry pie" to every question I ask you, but if you can, then you win a five pound note. (*She beams*)

Sir Rupert (*scornfully*) Don't be ridiculous. That's the stupidest game I've ever heard of. And besides — you haven't even got a five pound note.

Dame (*displaying the note*) Oh, yes, I have.

Sir Rupert (*suspiciously*) And I could win it by answering every question you ask me with the words "blackberry pie"?

Dame That's right.

Sir Rupert (*sneering*) You must be crackers. It'd be mine in no time.

Dame All right, then. Put your five pounds down there, (*she indicates a spot*) and I'll put mine next to it.

Sir Rupert gets out a fiver and places it on the indicated spot. The Dame puts hers on top of it

Now then … Are you ready?

Sir Rupert (*airily*) Whenever *you* are.

The Dame stoops and scoops up the money

(*Startled*) Just a minute. What are you *doing?*

Dame You didn't say "blackberry pie".

Sir Rupert (*annoyed*) But I didn't know we'd started. (*Firmly*) Put the money back down and we'll start again.

Dame Oh, no. A bet's a bet. If you want to try again it'll cost you another five pounds.

Sir Rupert What? (*Glowering*) Oh … very well, then. (*He puts another five pounds down*)

Dame places her five pounds on top of Sir Rupert's note

And this time you *won't* trick me.

Dame Right. Now you're quite sure you're ready?

Sir Rupert (*firmly*) Blackberry pie.

Dame You got it right, that time, didn't you?

Sir Rupert (*smirking*) Of course.

The Dame scoops up the money

Sir Rupert (*realizing*) Bah. She's done it again. (*Loudly*) I insist on a re-play. (*He gets out another fiver*)
Dame (*shrugging*) It's your money.

They place their bets again

Are you ready?
Sir Rupert (*firmly*) Blackberry pie.
Dame Is that your final answer?
Sir Rupert Blackberry pie.
Dame Do you think you're going to win, now?
Sir Rupert Blackberry pie.
Dame Which would you rather have? The money or a blackberry pie?
Sir Rupert (*smirking*) Blackberry pie.
Dame Well, in that case, *I'll* have the money. (*She quickly scoops the money up*)

The Dame exits DL

Sir Rupert (*startled*) What? (*He realizes*) Ohhhh—tricked again. (*Fuming*) I must get that money back, somehow. I know—I'll try the same thing on some other idiot. (*He glances around*) But who? And what's that notice doing over there? (*He moves towards the notice*)

Audience reaction

Dickie comes rushing on UR

Dickie Hiya, kids. (*To Sir Rupert*) Gerroff me notice-board, you sneaky snatcher. (*He recognizes Sir Rupert*) Oh—hallo, Sir Rupert. I didn't know it was you.
Sir Rupert (*scowling*) And where have you been all morning, you lacklustrous layabout? You were supposed to be mowing my beautiful lawns in time for the fête.
Dickie I know. But somebody'd bought me a real expensive present for my birthday, and I had to take it back to WH Smith's to tell 'em I didn't need it.
Sir Rupert Oh? And what was it?
Dickie One of those solar-powered pocket calculators.
Sir Rupert A solar-powered pocket calculator. (*Surprised*) And you didn't want it?

Dickie No.

Sir Rupert But why?

Dickie 'Cos I already *knew* how many pockets I had.

Sir Rupert (*after a reaction*) Yes ... Well I'm glad you've arrived, because I'm looking for someone like you to play a brand new game that could earn them a great deal of money. (*He gives a shark-like smile*)

Dickie (*interested*) Oooh. I think I'd like to play a game like that, Sir Rupert. How do you play it?

Sir Rupert (*smirking*) It's perfectly simple. I bet you five pounds that you can't say "blackberry pie" to every question I ask you — and if you can, then you get the money.

Dickie Blackberry pie?

Sir Rupert Blackberry pie.

Dickie (*grinning*) You're pulling my leg.

Sir Rupert No, I'm not.

Dickie (*amused*) You mean — you want to bet me *five pounds* I can't say "blackberry pie" to every question you ask me?

Sir Rupert That's right.

Dickie And if I can, then I win a fiver?

Sir Rupert That's correct.

Dickie (*delightedly*) It's money for old rope.

Sir Rupert Very well, then. Put your five pounds down there, and I'll put my five pounds on top of it.

The bets are placed

Now then — are you ready?

Dickie Blackberry pie.

Sir Rupert (*scowling, then trying again*) You got it right, that time, didn't you?

Dickie Blackberry pie.

Sir Rupert (*glowering, annoyed*)And you think you're going to win that money, don't you?

Dickie Blackberry pie.

Sir Rupert Well, which would you rather have? The money or a blackberry pie?

Dickie The money. (*He scoops it up quickly*)

Sir Rupert (*hastily*) Just a minute. Just a minute. You're not supposed to say *that*.

Dickie I know. But I've played this game before.

Dickie exits quickly UR

Sir Rupert (*furiously*) Come back.

Sir Rupert chases after Dickie and exits. The Fairy enters DR *in a white follow-spot*

Fairy (*frowning*) I cannot understand it. The whole thing's rather weird.
Attrocia's nowhere to be found. In fact, she's disappeared.
And yet I know that danger's near. There's menace in the air.
That wicked witch I have to find. But where's she hiding? Where?
(*She thinks*) Perhaps within the forest deep she's cunningly concealed?
If so, I cannot *rest* until her hiding place has been revealed.
For as our Queen, to ev'ry fairy, often has imparted,
To win, nip evil in the bud before it's even started.

The Fairy exits R

The follow-spot is extinguished

Hansel and Gretel enter UL *and move* DC

Hansel (*eagerly*) Now's our chance. They're all so busy enjoying themselves, no-one'll even notice we've slipped away to borrow more pebbles from the Mayor's drive.

Gretel (*protesting*) But we've still some left from yesterday. Why do we need more?

Hansel Because *this* time, we can go even *further* into the forest. (*Scornfully*) When we finished picking blackberries yesterday, we could still see the roof-tops.

Gretel (*remembering*) That's true. We couldn't have got lost if we'd tried.

Hansel And not only that... Because everyone in the village goes blackberry picking, there were only small ones left for us. If Aunt Dyspepsia's going to make a fortune selling pies, we need to find the great big sweet and juicy ones for her.

Gretel And you think we'll find them deeper in the forest?

Hansel (*firmly*) Of course, we will. The further away from the village they are, the less other people will go there to pick them.

Gretel (*eagerly*) So when shall we start?

Hansel As soon as we've filled our pockets with more pebbles. Come on.

They hurry off DR. *Lucy enters* UL, *glancing around*

Lucy Well — they're certainly not at this end of the gardens. (*She moves* DC, *a puzzled look on her face*) Where on earth can they be?

Karl enters DR

Karl Lucy. (*He moves to her*)

Lucy (*hastily*) I can't stay, Karl. Two of the children are missing. (*She glances round again*)
Karl Hansel and Gretel, you mean? (*He smiles*) It's all right. There's nothing to worry about. I've just seen them heading for the drive.
Lucy No, no. These are *village* children. No-one's seen them for *ages*.
Karl (*helpfully*) Maybe they're playing a game? You know? Like hide and seek
Lucy (*sighing*) They could be, I suppose. But their parents are getting quite worried.
Karl Well, I've plenty of free time this morning so *I* can help you search, if you'd like?
Lucy If only we knew where to start.

There is a commotion off R *and Potz and Panz enter* DR, *each firmly holding a wriggling and protesting Hansel and Gretel*

Hansel (*fiercely*) Let go of me. Let go.
Gretel (*calling*) Help. Help.

The Villagers and Guests hurry on UL *and* UR

Villagers (*variously*) What's happening? What's wrong? (*Etc.*)
Karl (*to Potz and Panz, firmly*) Unhand those children at once.
Potz Not likely. We caught 'em filling their pockets with pebbles from the Mayor's drive.
Panz Yes. And now we're going to find out what he has to say about it.
Karl (*to the children*) Is this true?
Hansel (*defensively*) We were only *borrowing* them.
Gretel To make sure that we wouldn't get lost
Lucy (*to Potz and Panz*) Well, I'm sure Sir Rupert's got more to worry about than children taking pebbles from his drive.

The Villagers agree with nods and murmurs

Potz Not according to him, he hasn't. He lost sixty yesterday.
Karl (*scornfully*) And how could he possibly know that? There must be millions of them down there.
Panz (*confidently*) Four million, thirty-six thousand, eight hundred and ninety-two. (*Grimacing*) He had us *counting* 'em till half-past three this morning.
Lucy But there's no need to bother him with a silly thing like this. You could let them go if they promise never to do it again.

Hansel and Gretel nod in agreement

Potz (*reluctantly*) Well — I suppose we could. But if we do, you mustn't let him find out. Now he's the Chief Magistrate as well, he's been handing out some very funny punishments.

Panz (*agreeing*) Not half. He had an old age pensioner in court last week for pinching a tin of tomatoes from (*local supermarket*). And do you know what he did to her?

Karl I've no idea.

Potz He opened the *tin* to see how many tomatoes were inside it, then sent her to jail for six months. One month for every tomato.

Karl (*startled*) And what did she say to that?

Panz Thank goodness she'd changed her mind in time and put the baked beans back.

Lucy (*hopefully*) So you *will* let them go?

Potz (*agreeing*) Oh, go on then.

The Bailiffs release Hansel and Gretel who hurry to Lucy's side

Panz (*sternly*) But they mustn't do it again. 'Cos the next time we catch 'em, it's our solemn duty as protectors of the peace to see they get what's coming to 'em. Isn't that right, Potz?

Potz It certainly is.

Song 7 (*Potz and Panz*)

As the song progresses, others may join in with appropriate dance steps. At the end of the song there is a general high-spirited reception from all and the scene ends in a atmosphere of gaiety

Black-out

Scene 4

The Edge of the Great Forest

A lane scene depicting a country lane with dense forestry in the background. The lighting is subdued

Attrocia enters L *in a green light*

Attrocia (*gleefully*) With joy, my wicked heart is filled;
My plan has worked a treat.
There's nothing children can resist
That's *bad* for them, or sickly *sweet*.
Like wasps around a jam-pot
They'll appear, but find instead

Of feasting on the things they *like*,
They're turned to tasty *gingerbread.*
(*Sweetly*) So come, you darling kiddi-winks —
In ones or twos or threes —
When friends call round to visit me,
I'll proudly serve you — for their *teas.* (*She cackles*)

Attrocia exits L

The green light goes out and the Lights return to their Scene 3 setting

The Dame enters R, *in another extraordinary costume*

Dame (*to the audience*) Oh, I say … (*She glances upwards*) That was a bit of a black cloud. I thought it was going to rain. Mind you — we need it, don't we? It's weeks since we had any. The garden looks terrible and they're no help at all at the weather bureau. I rang 'em last night to see if there was any chance of a shower, and the feller at the other end said "Don't worry, missis. If you're that dirty, have one." (*She glances* DL) Oh, I say … what a peculiar notice board. (*Reading*) "Do not ring this bell." (*Puzzled*) I wonder what it means. I'll give it a ring and find out. (*She moves toward the notice*)

The audience reacts

Dickie dashes in R

Dickie Hiya, kids. (*To the Dame*) Get your hands off my dinger. (*He recognizes her*) Oh, hallo, Dyspepsia. I didn't know it was you. I thought it was somebody trying to pinch me button-board.

Dame (*tartly*) Never mind your button-board. You were supposed to meet me outside (*local café or tea shop*) nearly an hour ago. Where've you been?

Dickie (*protesting*) It wasn't my fault. I was just on my way there when this ambulance came screeching round the corner doing sixty miles an hour — and the next thing I knew, I was being rushed to hospital.

Dame (*shocked*) They hadn't knocked you down, had they?

Dickie No. I'd got me braces hooked on the wing mirror.

Dame (*put out*) Yes — well, you want to think yourself lucky I didn't go off with somebody else while I was waiting. You're not the only one round here who fancies me, you know. (*She smirks*)

Dickie (*startled*) Eh?

Dame You see him, down there? (*She indicates loosely into the audience*) The feller in the fifth row with the sketching pad and pencil.

Dickie (*peering*) Yes. (*Puzzled*) But how do you know he fancies you?

Dame Because he's been drawing my picture for the last ten minutes. I think he must be an artist. (*She poses archly and simpers*)

Dickie (*peering again*) No, he's not, Dyspi. I recognize him, now. His photo was in the (*local paper*) last week. He's not an artist. He's a famous designer.

Dame (*delightedly*) You mean he designs glamorous frocks for beautiful women? And that's why he's drawing me?

Dickie No, no. He designs door-knockers.

Dame (*hurt*) I might have known you'd spoil everything. You haven't a romantic bone in your body.

Dickie (*protesting*) Yes, I have. If we got married, I'd climb the highest mountains, cross the widest deserts and swim the deepest seas for you.

Dame Well, there's not much point in getting married, then, is there? You'd never be at home.

Dickie (*coaxing*) Oh, come on, Dyspi. Tell me you'll marry me

Dame Well if I *do*, you've got to promise you'll still love me when I'm old and ugly.

Dickie Don't worry, Dyspi. You might grow *older*, but in *my* eyes, you could never grow *uglier*.

Dame (*flattered*) Flatterer.

Song 8 (*Dickie and Dame*)

At the end of the song they exit L. *As they do so, Hansel and Gretel enter* R

Hansel (*downcast*) It's not fair. All that fuss over a few stupid pebbles. Now we can't go into the forest — and Aunt Dyspepsia'll never get rich.

Gretel If only we could help *another* way.

Hansel (*hotly*) But what we were doing was far the easiest. Everyone likes blackberry pie and nobody bakes them like her. She's the best cook in the whole wide world.

Gretel (*thoughtfully*) We could use something different to make a trail with.

Hansel (*gloomily*) Like what, for instance?

Gretel (*after a moment*) Pieces of twig?

Hansel (*scornfully*) I don't think they'd be much help. The forest floor's covered with them. It'd have to be something we'd notice at once.

Gretel How about — breadcrumbs? (*Eagerly*) There's a whole loaf of stale bread in the pantry and I'm sure she won't miss a few slices.

Hansel (*brightening*) And it wouldn't be as heavy as pebbles. It's the very thing. Quick. Let's get back to the village.

They hurry off L, *excitedly. Potz and Panz enter* R

Potz Ooooh, I'm starving, aren't you? I've had nothing to eat all day.

Panz (*surprised*) What about your breakfast?

Potz I didn't have any. You know I can't eat on an empty stomach.

Panz Well, we can't go looking for missing pebbles if you're moaning and groaning all the time. Let's go back to the village and you can have something to eat at (*local café*). They do chicken dinners there for only twenty p.

Potz (*amazed*) Twenty p? For a chicken dinner? How can they make a profit doing that?

Panz Well it doesn't cost much for a handful of *corn,* does it?

Potz (*grimacing*) Oh, I'm fed up of working for the Mayor. We've only been doing it for two days and half the villagers won't even talk to us.

Panz (*glumly*) I know. And now we've to go in the forest looking for his missing pebbles. I wish I hadn't left my old job.

Potz Well why did you?

Panz Because of illness. The boss got sick of me.

Potz Ooooh, it's funny that. 'Cos I left my old job through illness, as well. I could hardly stand up straight 'cos of the pain in my back. I had violent headaches every morning, my hair was falling out, I couldn't sleep, my eyes wouldn't stop watering, my nose was always running and my circulation was that bad, I had pins and needles all over my body.

Panz (*amazed*) Where did you work?

Potz In a health food shop.

Panz snatches off his hat and beats Potz around the shoulders with it

Panz Go back to the village and get something to eat. (*He puts his hat back on*) I'll sit on the fence over there (*he indicates off* L) and wait for you.

Potz OK. I won't be long.

Potz exits R. *Sir Rupert enters* L

Sir Rupert Ah, there you are, Bailiff Panz. Just the man I'm looking for. Remember that two pounds I paid you in advance yesterday? Well, I appear to have left my wallet behind and need the money back immediately. (*Aside*) It's an old trick, but it never fails. No-one gets money out of *me.* (*He smirks*)

Panz (*flustered*) But I haven't got any money, Mr Mayor. I spent it on food.

Sir Rupert (*scowling*) In that case, I'm afraid I'll have to sack you. (*Aside*) Which means I won't have to fork out his wages at the end of the week (*He chuckles gleefully*)

Panz (*hastily*) Wait a minute though. I might be able to borrow it from somebody. (*To the Musical Director*) Excuse me ...

Sir Rupert (*puzzled*) Who are you talking to? (*He glances around*)

Panz The musical director. He/She's a lovely feller/woman. Has the best three-piece band in the country. It should have been a twelve-piece, really, but the others couldn't get bail. (*To the Musical Director*) Er ... Can you lend me a couple of pounds, (*he names the MD*)?

Musical Director Sorry, Panzi — I've only got a pound coin on me.

Panz Well, can you lend me that then?

The coin is passed up to Panz

Ta. (*To Sir Rupert*) Right. Well I haven't got two pounds, but I can give you one back and owe you the other.

Sir Rupert (*scowling*) Oh, very well. But don't think I'm likely to forget.

Panz (*downcast*) No, no. I wouldn't think that. (*He hands over the money*) There's one pound and I still owe you another.

Panz exits gloomily L

Sir Rupert (*smirking*) Another pound returned to the coffers. If I invest this in a mini-cash ISA, I'll get the interest on it and not pay a penny in income tax. (*He chuckles*)

Potz enters R

Potz Oooh, I'm still starving. I'd got all the way down to the village before I found out I hadn't any money and ... (*He sees Sir Rupert*) Ooooh, the very feller. (*He hurries to him*) Remember that two pounds you borrowed from me this morning, Mr Mayor? Well, I need it back straight away.

Sir Rupert (*aghast*) What? Can't I give it to you later? (*Blustering*) I seem to have lost my wallet and don't have two pounds on me. I've only got one.

Potz (*cheerfully*) Well, that's all right. You can give me the one, and owe me the other.

Sir Rupert (*beaten*) Oh, very well. (*He hands over the coin*) But don't think I'll take this lying down.

Sir Rupert exits L *in a temper*

Potz (*happily*) Now to head back to the village for something to eat.

Panz enters L

Panz Oh, you're back, are you?

Potz Yes. But I'm not stopping. Now I've got some money, I'm heading back to the village for dinner. (*He heads for the exit* R)

Panz (*quickly*) Hang on a minute. Hang on. If you've got some money, you can pay me back the two pounds you owe me. (*He holds his hand out*)

Potz No, I can't. I haven't got two pounds. I've only got one.

Panz Well, you'd better give me that then, and you can still owe me the other.

Potz (*mournfully*) Bang goes my surprise pie. (*He hands over the coin*)

Panz Surprise pie?

Potz It's the special offer at (*local café*).

Panz And what's in it?

Potz Chicken.

Panz (*puzzled*) So what's the surprise?

Potz The chef forgot to take the feathers off it.

Panz (*beaming*) Well, now I've got some money, I might have a slice of pie myself.

Sir Rupert enters L

Sir Rupert Did someone mention money? (*He smirks*) Well, don't forget, you still owe me a pound. (*He holds out his hand*)

Panz (*groaning*) Oh, no. (*He hands the pound over*) Well, that makes us square.

Sir Rupert (*smirking*) Indeed it does.

Potz And *you* still owe *me* a pound, don't you, Mr Mayor? (*He holds out his hand*)

Sir Rupert (*scowling*) Bed-bugs and gnat-bites. I thought he'd forget. (*He hands it over unhappily*) Well, that makes us square.

Panz And *you* owed *me* a pound, didn't you, Potzi? (*He holds out his hand*)

Potz (*handing the pound over*) So that makes *us* square.

Panz And if I give the pound back to (*he names the MD*) that *I* owed, (*he does so*) that makes *us* square.

Potz
Panz } (*together*) Bye-bye, Sir Rupert.

Potz and Panz exit L *rapidly, leaving Sir Rupert fuming. He storms after them*

The Lights fade rapidly

Scene 5

A Clearing in the Forest

A three-quarter set with a backdrop depicting thick forestry. This cloth should be on a track enabling it to open centrally, or to be flown. DS *of this drop, trees mask entrances and exits* L *and* R *and a fallen log, which doubles as a seat, is* UL. C *in the space behind the cloth is the gingerbread house, a colourful, mouth-watering construction of confectionery, with barley-sugar windows, icing-sugared walls and gingerbread slates, decorated with iced buns and liquorice allsorts etc., and with a practical door. The whole building must look good enough to eat. A white picket-fence with a central opening is in front of this and giant lollipops substitute for trees in the garden. A huge chocolate swiss roll acts as a seat by the door. Behind the house is a backdrop of thick forest*

When the scene begins, the light is diffused but not gloomy; it slowly fades as the scene continues

The clearing is occupied by a group of Gypsies in colourful costumes. Melindra, their Queen, is seated on the log, whilst others stand around in groups watching a troupe of Gypsy Dancers

Song and Dance 9 (*Gypsies*)

At the end of the song the Gypsy Audience applauds the Dancers

The Dancers exit L

Roderigo enters DR

Melindra (*rising*) Have the children returned, Roderigo?
Roderigo Not yet, Melindra. But there's nothing to worry about. They know the forest like the backs of their hands.

The others agree with nods and murmurs

Melindra (*concerned*) But daylight is fading and no-one has seen them for hours.
Roderigo (*amused*) They play in the streams and hide among the trees. When hunger strikes, they'll be first to arrive at the fireside.
Melindra (*smiling*) You're probably right. But somehow I feel that the forest has changed. Yesterday, the wild creatures moved among us without fear. Today they take flight at the slightest sound.
Roderigo (*shrugging*) Perhaps a storm is brewing?
Melindra If so, we'd better look for the children before it arrives. For so many to leave our camp all day, it's almost unheard of.
Roderigo Then search for them we will. (*Lightly*) But with so many berries on the bushes, I suspect quite a few of our little ragamuffins will not be wanting supper tonight. (*He bows*)

Roderigo exits R, *jauntily*

The others laugh and exit variously

Melindra (*looking upwards in concern*) The sky darkens and already the moon is rising. I must tend to the fire and hope that they quickly return.

Melindra exits UL

There is a pause

Gretel (*off* R; *calling*) This way, Hansel. This way.

Gretel hurries on UR

Hurry. (*She stops* C *and looks anxiously around the floor of the clearing*)

Hansel enters UR, *carrying the pail of blackberries and protesting*

Hansel Don't *walk* so fast. I've already spilled *some* of them. (*He notices her*) What's wrong?

Gretel (*uneasily*) It's getting too dark. I can't see them anywhere.

Hansel The crumbs, you mean? Are you sure we're on the right path?

Gretel Of course, we are. (*Doubtfully*) I think. (*She looks round again*)

Hansel (*looking around the clearing*) I don't remember *this* place.

Gretel (*firmly*) *I* do. (*She indicates* L) There's the bush you scratched your leg on. (*Uncertainly*) Or was it that one? (*She indicates another*)

Hansel (*putting the pail down*) Let's get on our hands and knees. We're sure to find the breadcrumbs if we're close enough.

They get to their knees and search in vain

I can't see anything.

Gretel (*protesting*) But I left a trail, Hansel. I did. I did.

Hansel I know. (*A little afraid*) But it's not there now.

Gretel What can have happened to them?

Hansel (*at a loss*) Perhaps they've been blown away — or eaten by birds?

Gretel (*horrified*) Oh, no. I'd forgotten that birds like crumbs. (*Worried*) Oh, Hansel. Does that mean we're lost?

Hansel (*bravely*) Of course it doesn't. We just — don't know where we are.

Gretel We could be here for ever and *ever*.

Hansel (*dismissively*) No, we couldn't. If it wasn't so dark, we could probably see the church steeple from here.

Gretel (*anxiously*) Should we go on a little bit further?

Hansel I don't see why not. (*He stands*) It's just a case of deciding which way to go.We don't want to walk in the wrong direction.

Gretel (*miserably*) I wish we'd listened to Aunt Dyspepsia and never come into the forest. She must be so worried about us.

Hansel I expect she is. (*Brightly*) But she won't be cross when she sees all the berries we've picked.

Gretel But what if she *never* sees them? What if we're lost in the forest like those poor little Babes in the Wood?

Hansel (*brightly*) Then we'll just have to wait for Robin Hood and his men to come along and find us.

Gretel Oh, Hansel. I'm frightened.

Hansel There's nothing to be scared of. Honestly. I'm sure we can find our way back without a trail of mouldy old breadcrumbs. Shall we try?

Gretel I'd rather stay here till the moon's a bit brighter. (*She yawns tiredly*)

Hansel Then that's what we'll do. We can rest at the side of this log, (*he indicates it*) and you can even go to sleep if you like. I'll waken you up when it's light enough.

Gretel If you're sure you don't mind.

Hansel Of course I don't.

They settle down at the side of the log and Gretel curls up to sleep

(*After a moment*) And you needn't worry about me going to sleep. I'm not the least bit tired. I can stay awake all night if I have to. (*Yawning*) I don't really need to sleep at all. (*Yawning again*) I could probably stay awake forever — if I wanted … (*His voice trails away and he too falls asleep*)

The effect of moonlight comes up on the scene

The Fairy appears R *in a white follow-spot*

Fairy Throughout the forest wide I've searched and found not e'en a trace
Of wicked witch, Attrocia. Where has she made her hiding place?
And all those missing boys and girls — I'm certain she's to blame.
But rest assured, whate'er she's planned, I'll quickly spoil her nasty game.
(*She notices Hansel and Gretel*)
What's this? Two little children. All alone and deep in sleep?
With no-one near to guard them or a watchful eye to keep?
Poor mortals. Tired and frightened. They're lost without a doubt.
I'll bring them help. (*She hesitates*) And yet, I fear — Attrocia is still about
But magic will protect them, so no harm can come their way,
And pleasant thoughts shall fill their dreams until the breaking of the day.
(*She waves her wand over them*)

The Fairy exits R

The white follow-spot is extinguished. A moment later there is a fanfare and music begins

Music 10. Dream sequence (*Company*)

Into the clearing marches a team of white mice in silver and red waistcoats, each mouse holding a lighted lantern which increases the general lighting. They take up positions around the exterior of the clearing. Once there, a procession of fairy tale characters appears: Snow White and the Dwarfs, Alice and the Wonderland characters, Cinderella and the Ugly Sisters, etc. They parade around the clearing then take up their positions as Fairies appear and perform a graceful and dreamy ballet. At the end of the dance, the Lights fade to Black-out and everyone apart from Hansel and Gretel melts away to exit in total darkness

In the black-out, the backdrop is flown or drawn away

The Lights come up to full daylight and the gingerbread house is revealed. A cockerel crows loudly and Hansel and Gretel awake. As they get to their feet and see the house, they move C, *in awe, their backs to the audience*

Hansel (*awed*) Do you see what I see, Gretel?
Gretel (*awed*) It's a Gingerbread House.

The two children hold hands and slowly move US

There is a soft, sinister chuckle from Attrocia on an off-stage microphone

CURTAIN

ACT II

Scene 1

Back at the Village

The set is as Act I Scene 1, with full lighting

Once again the Villagers are singing and dancing

Song 11 (*Villagers*)

After the song, Lucy hurries in UL

Villager 1 (*cheerily*) Good-morning, Lucy. What are you doing here so early? Run out of milk for the Mayor's breakfast? (*Amused*) Most of the shops aren't open, yet.

Villager 2 (*teasing*) It's not shops she's looking for. It's a certain young forester who'll be passing through the village in the next few minutes on his way to work.

The Villagers react amusedly

Lucy As a matter of fact, you're both wrong. I came to see if anyone had found the missing children.

The Villagers look surprised

Villager 1 What would *we* know about *gypsy* children? They've not been seen in *our* village.

The Villagers agree

Lucy (*surprised*) Gypsy children?

Villager 2 Their parents came looking for them, late last night. And the Gypsy Queen promised a reward to anyone who found them. (*Impressed*) One hundred pieces of gold.

Lucy (*worried*) Oh, no.

Villager 1 (*puzzled*) Is something wrong?

Lucy Haven't you *heard?* There are *village* children missing, too. They vanished from the fête yesterday afternoon.
Villager 2 (*shocked*) No-one told *us*. We know nothing about it.

The Villagers agree

But there's nothing to worry about. No-one comes to harm in our Kingdom. The Forest Fairy sees to that.

The Villagers agree

Villager 1 They're probably hiding in the forest for a joke.

The Villagers agree

Lucy (*uncertainly*) Perhaps you're right. But I shan't be happy till I know they've turned up again.
Villager 2 Don't worry, Lucy. If they're not back by lunchtime, we'll all go out to search for them.

The Villagers agree

Lucy Then I'd better get back to Siezitt Hall before Sir Rupert finds out I've gone. But the minute you hear anything, please let me know.
Villager 1 We will.

Lucy exits UL. *The Villagers exit variously. When the last of them has gone, Potz and Panz enter* UL, *and move* DC

Panz (*worried*) What are we going to *do,* Potzi? The Mayor'll go crackers when he hears we haven't found his precious pebbles.
Panz (*smugly*) No, he won't. Because he'll never know, will he? Why do you think I told you to go home last night and get some sleep?
Panz I don't know. But I wish you hadn't. It was so dark when I walked past the wishing well, I tripped up and fell down it.
Potz (*amazed*) You fell down the wishing well? But it's sixty metres deep. (*Alarmed*) You didn't break anything, did you?
Panz (*scornfully*) 'Course not. There was nothing down there to break.

Potz reacts, then snatches off his hat and beats Panz about the shoulders with it

(*Cowering*) Owww. Owww. Owww.

Potz (*annoyed*) Now stop messing about and listen. (*He replaces his hat*) What did the Mayor say we had to do if we didn't want him to sack us?

Panz (*remembering with an effort*) Go into the forest, find the pebbles Hansel and Gretel pinched from his drive and bring 'em all back again. (*He looks triumphant*)

Potz And how many did we find?

Panz (*thinking*) Er ... (*He counts rapidly on his fingers, face contorting with concentration*) None.

Potz So what are we going to do?

Panz Find another job. (*He turns to exit*)

Potz (*grabbing hold of him*) No, we are not. (*Patiently*) We're going to buy sixty pebbles from (*local builders' merchants*) and tell the old miser we recovered the lot. That way we needn't go into the forest again and we still keep our jobs. (*He smirks*)

Panz (*looking around*) So where's the builders' shop, then?

Potz I don't know. But there's a big *button* over there. We'll press *that* and see if it belongs to *him*.

Potz and Panz move towards the button

The audience reacts

Dickie rushes on UR

Dickie Hiya, kids. (*To Potz and Panz*) Gerroff me button. You pilferous pair.

Panz (*flustered*) We were only going to ring for the builder.

Dickie (*suspiciously*) Yes. Well he wouldn't hear you ringing that. He's gone out jogging.

Potz Jogging? (*He glances at Panz in alarm*)

Dickie (*nodding*) He wanted to add a few years to his life, and his doctor said the best way of doing it was to stop eating junk food and get more exercise.

Panz (*curiously*) And is it working?

Dickie 'Course it is. I asked him this morning. He said he felt ten years older already. (*He chortles*)

Potz Well it's no use hanging about if he's not in, so we'd better get going. Hadn't we, Panz? (*He indicates with a twitch of his head*)

Panz (*blankly*) Had we?

Potz (*gritting his teeth*) Of course we have. We're going to turn the radio on and listen to a match.

Panz (*indignantly*) No we're *not* ... The last time *I* listened to a match I burnt my ear.

Potz reacts, snatches off his hat and beats Panz with it and they exit DL

Dickie (*to the audience*) They get dafter, those two. Here … and talking about daft things. Have you heard the latest? Sir Rupert's given fifty thousand pounds to (*present political party leader*) so his party can have a new lavatory built in the Houses of Parliament. (*Incredulously*) Fifty thousand pounds. (*Shrugging*) Still — I suppose they've got to have one place where they know what they're doing. (*He sighs deeply*) But it's Dyspi I'm worried about. She's acting ever so strange, lately. (*Confidentially*) I went round to her cottage last week and we were sitting on the sofa watching *Emmerdale* (*or other television programme*) … when suddenly she jumped to her feet, rushed over to the television, pulled the plug out, closed the curtains and switched off all the lights. (*He looks surprised*) Well, I'm not daft, you know. I can take a hint as well as anybody. So I went home and let her go to bed.

Karl enters UR, *looking concerned*

Karl (*glancing around*) Where is everyone?

Dickie No use asking me. Somebody left a gate open in Farmer Brown's field last week and all his cows got out. I've been helping him look for 'em all morning.

Karl Has he advertised in the (*local newspaper*)?

Dickie (*scornfully*) Don't be daft. Cows can't read. (*Puzzled*) But what are you looking so worried about?

Karl (*uneasily*) I've just heard some rather strange news. There are children missing from every village in the forest.

Dickie (*surprised*) Oo-er. You don't think something's happened to 'em, do you?

Karl (*amused*) Of course not. Since the Fairies promised their protection hundreds of years ago, there's never been anything serious enough for us to worry about. (*Frowning*) It's just odd, that's all.

Dickie (*wide-eyed*) But what if they're in the *forest?* It's only in the *villages* we're protected.

Karl Because there's nothing in the forest to do us any harm. No bears. No wolves. No dragons. It's as safe as our own back gardens.

Dickie It's not safe in *my* back garden. I was out there a few minutes ago and a dirty great wasp came buzzing along and stung me on one of me fingers.

Karl (*glancing at Dickie's hands*) Which one?

Dickie I haven't a clue. All wasps look the same to me.

There is a loud wail off R, *and Dame Do-Good comes hurrying on in a panic*

Dame Quick. Quick. Somebody help. (*Looking around*) I can't find 'em anywhere. (*She bursts into tears*)

Karl (*startled*) Find who?

Dame Hansel and Gretel. They've gone. Vanished. I've been searching for 'em all night. (*She sobs loudly*)

Dickie (*valiantly*) Don't worry, Dyspepsia. I'll find 'em for you.

Dame (*scornfully*) You? You couldn't find the front of a queue if you were the only one *in* it. (*She continues to sob*)

Dickie (*reasonably*) Well they can't have gone far, can they? They've only got little legs.

Karl (*frowning*) And there's the other missing children, too.

Dame (*stopping crying*) Eh??? What others?

Karl Quite a lot of them. (*To Dickie*) Perhaps you're right, Dickie? Maybe they *are* in the forest.

Dame What are they doing *there?*

Karl (*shrugging*) Camping out, I suppose.

Dickie (*eagerly*) Oooh, yes. You can have smashing fun doing that. (*Proudly*) I was in the Sea Scouts when I was little and we had fantastic times till we had to pack it in.

Karl Why was that?

Dickie All the tents sank.

Dame (*annoyed*) Never mind him and his Sea Scouts. (*Anguished*) What about Hansel and Gretel? How do we find them?

The Fairy enters R *in a white spot*

Karl (*taken aback*) The Forest Fairy. (*He removes his hat and bows deeply*)

Dame and Dickie bow and curtsy confusedly

Fairy Within the forest, vast and deep, those you seek, in safety, sleep.
Protected by a fairy charm to keep them well and free from harm.
A primrose path shall be your guide and lead you swiftly to their side.

Dame (*greatly relieved*) Oh, thank goodness for that. I'll make 'em the best breakfast they've ever had. (*Remembering*) And I'll bake some fairy cakes as well. Especially for you.

Fairy (*smiling*) Alas, I have no time to stay. I really must be on my way.
A wicked witch hides somewhere near who threatens all that you hold dear.
But rest assured, she'll quickly find I've ways of dealing with *her* kind.
Her puny pow'rs shall not withstand the awesome might of Fairyland.
(*She waves her wand*)

The Fairy exits R

The white spot is extinguished

Karl (*calling after her*) Wait ... (*To the others*) She's gone. And we never had time to ask if the other children were there, too.

Dickie (*awed*) No. But did you hear *that?* She's going to fight a *witch.*

Karl I never knew they still existed.

Dame (*knowingly*) Oh, yes. One of 'em used to advertise in "Yours" magazine. (*Recites*) "Winnie the Witch. Curses a speciality." I wrote to her myself, once.

Karl (*staring at her*) Whatever for?

Dame To see what she'd charge to frighten that nasty old Mayor of ours.

Dickie And what did she say?

Dame She said "Send me ten pounds and I'll frighten him out of his wits". So I got me cheque-book out and sent her *five*.

Karl (*puzzled*) Five?

Dame Well ... he's only a *half*-wit, isn't he? (*Excitedly*) But never mind that. Now we know where Hansel and Gretel are, we can go and collect 'em. (*She moves* DR *as if to exit*) I'll just pop home and make us a few sandwiches for the journey.

Karl (*quickly*) There's no need for that. They can't be more than a mile or two away, and I know the forest like the back of my hand. You spread the news that we've found them, and I'll have them here in no time.

Dickie (*agreeing*) It's a good idea, Dyspi. We don't want you tripping on a tree root and breaking your leg again. Last time you did it, the doctor stopped you using stairs, didn't he? And it was six weeks before he took your plaster-cast off

Dame (*remembering*) Oooh, yes. And wasn't I glad when he did? It used to wear me out, shinning up that drainpipe to get to bed.

Karl (*interrupting*) Well I'd best be on my way. They'll be waking up soon, and I'd like to be there before they do. The sight of a friendly face should more than make up for a night in the forest — and with a bit of luck they'll be home before you've had time to cook their breakfast.

Song 12 (*Karl*)

The Villagers enter variously as Karl sings

Dickie and the Dame rapidly "spread the news" as he sings, then all join in

At the end of the song, Karl exits UR

The others wave Karl off

The Lights fade rapidly to Black-out

SCENE 2

Outside Siezitt Hall

A lane scene

The Lights come up to full

Sir Rupert enters L, *in a temper*

Sir Rupert Bah. Still no trace of my missing pebbles, and those bungling bailiffs are nowhere to be found. Just wait till I get my hands on 'em.

Potz and Panz enter R, *beaming*

Potz (*cheerfully*) Looking for us, boss?
Sir Rupert (*scowling*) And where do you think you've been all morning?
Panz (*surprised*) You told us you wanted something *special* for tonight's dinner. So we went to the river to do some fly fishing.
Sir Rupert (*remembering*) Ah, yes. Of course. And did you *catch* anything?
Potz Yes. A four pound blue-bottle.

Potz and Panz fall about. Sir Rupert scowls

Panz Mind you — I don't think there's any fish in that river. Jamie Oliver (*or other celebrity chef*) was down there trying to catch salmon, and offered fifty pounds to anybody who'd help him.
Sir Rupert (*incredulously*) Fifty pounds?
Potz Yes. He said he hadn't had a bite all day.
Sir Rupert So what did you do?
Panz We bit him.

Potz and Panz fall about again

Sir Rupert Bah. Well, never mind fish for dinner. I've just heard there's a big reward for finding those missing gypsy children. (*Gleefully*) One hundred pieces of gold. So while *I* go search for *them*, you two get cracking and find those missing pebbles of mine
Potz (*groaning*) Oh, we're not back to them again, are we?
Sir Rupert (*scowling*) Yes, you are. And you're going to stay with them till they're all returned. Pebbles cost money, and money is the only thing that interests me. Big, big, money. (*He rubs his finger and thumb*)
Panz My Uncle Fred went to jail for making big money.
Sir Rupert Don't be ridiculous. How could he be sent to jail for making big money?
Panz It was fifty centimetres too big.
Sir Rupert Bah.

Song 13 (*Sir Rupert, Potz and Panz*)

At the end of the song, they all exit L. *Lucy hurries on* R, *looking very worried*

Lucy I must find Karl. There are more children missing since yesterday. If we don't find out why, there'll be none left at all.

The Lights begin to dim

(*Surprised*) What's happening? (*She glances upwards, off* L, *and reacts in shock*) A witch. Riding on her broomstick and heading this way. What can she want here? I'd better hide before she sees me.

Lucy exits R, *hastily*

The Lights dim

Attrocia enters L, *in a green follow-spot. She has a broomstick*

Attrocia (*in triumph*) A fig for fairies and their spells;
For mortal hisses, boos and yells.
(*She smirks*) Without a doubt, you can't deny,
The vilest witch on earth am I.
(*Gleefully*) How tempting is my cottage sweet.
For little children, quite a treat.
With cream-cake walls — and overhead —
Thick shingles made of gingerbread.
Liquorice all-sorts chimney pots,
Plus M & Ms and Jelly Tots.
Doors of fudge and candy canes;
Barley-sugar window-panes.
Jammy tarts and chocolate slabs.
Marshmallows, crisps and sherbert dabs.
An endless, nauseating list
Of goodies children can't resist …
But once they're trapped — as I intend —
I'll bring them to a sticky end. (*She sniggers*)
So back to where those treats I share
With whosoever ventures there.
(*She shrieks in delight*)

Attrocia exits L. *The green light is extinguished and the lighting returns to normal*

Lucy enters R

Lucy (*gazing after her*) So that's where the missing children are. Trapped by a witch inside a house made of cakes and sweets. (*Aghast*) I've got to find help at once.

Lucy hurries off R

The Lights rapidly fade to Black-out

Scene 3

Outside the Gingerbread House

A full set. The backdrop of forest remains as in Scene 5, but the DS *log seat and picket fence have gone; we are in the garden of the gingerbread house. The avenue of lollipops flanking the house has been brought forward, and shrubs glistening with foil-wrapped sweets conceal entrances and exits* L *and* R*. The Lighting is warm and full*

Hansel and Gretel are standing DC*, still holding hands, their backs to the audience, drinking in the sight*

Hansel (*awed*) It's not really *there*, is it? We *are* dreaming?

Gretel (*dazed*) Walls of cake. Roof of gingerbread. Windows of barley sugar. Oh, Hansel … It makes my mouth water just *looking* at it.

Hansel (*deciding*) There's only *one* way to find out. (*He releases her hand and hurries up to the house*) I'll try a piece of barley sugar. (*He takes a twist from the window, licks at it and reacts with delight*) Well, that settles it. We *are* dreaming.

Gretel What makes you so sure?

Hansel Because nothing real could ever taste *this* good. (*He licks at the barley sugar stick again*) And where else but in a dream would you find a house made of cakes and sweets? Of course we're dreaming.

Gretel (*glancing around*) But it seems so *real*.

Hansel Then make the most of it before we wake up. Have a piece of window-sill. It's cream-cake sprinkled with icing sugar.

Gretel cautiously takes a corner of window-sill and tastes it

Gretel (*amazed*) Mmmmmm. (*She eats eagerly*)

Hansel (*looking at the cottage*) I wonder who it belongs to?

Gretel I don't know. But I'm glad we're dreaming about it. Aunt Dyspi's porridge is *lovely*, but I'd *much* rather have *cake* for breakfast. Oh, *do* try some of this. (*She offers him some cake*)

Hansel No, thanks. But I *will* have some of that gingerbread roof. (*He reaches for a piece*)

Attrocia (*voice-over on an off-stage microphone; sweetly*)

Nibble, nibble, little mouse.
Who's that nibbling at my house?

Hansel and Gretel react, in shock

Gretel (*whispering*) It must be the person who *lives* here.
Hansel (*recovering*) Don't worry. It's just a part of the dream. If we answer, they'll soon go away. (*Calling, in a dreamy voice*) It is the *wind,* the wind so *wild.* The *restless* wind. The heavenly *child.*

They giggle helplessly, then resume eating

The door opens and Attrocia appears in the opening, disguised as an old peasant woman leaning on a gnarled walking-stick. She emerges and moves behind them

Attrocia (*in a sweet, quavery tones*) Well, bless my soul. I do declare.
It's little children feasting there.

Hansel and Gretel turn to face Attrocia and recoil

(*Reassuringly*) No need to fear. You're welcome thrice,
To eat your fill of all that's nice.
From Jaffa cakes to sweets galore —
Whate'er you choose, there's plenty more. (*She smiles*)
Gretel (*nervously*) Who are *you*?
Attrocia (*sweetly*) A friend to those, I'm glad to say,
Who from well-trodden footpaths stray;
As, once my cottage quaint they've found,
I guide them homewards, safe and sound.
Hansel (*doubtfully*) You mean — you could show us the way to Pumpernickel if we asked you?
Attrocia Of *course* I could. (*Coaxing*) But ere I *do*,
I've special treats to show to you
Inside my house. So come and see.
Most surely, you'll be safe with me. (*She leers*)
Gretel (*uncomfortable*) I don't think we should. Even if we are only dreaming. Aunt Dyspepsia says we mustn't go anywhere with strangers.
Attrocia (*delightedly*) Dyspepsia? Why, goodness me. My very dearest friend.
Once ev'ry month she visits me, a little time to spend.
How pleased she'll be to know you're here. I'll call her right away.
What fun we'll have when she arrives. What jolly games we'll play.
We'll dine on cakes and lollipops; drink fizzy lemonade.
So step inside. You won't regret the happy day you strayed. (*She indicates the open door*)

Hansel (*suspiciously*) It's very kind of you, but we'll stay out here if you don't mind. Aunt Dyspi says too much sugar isn't good for us.
Attrocia (*hastily*) How very true. I quite agree.
My mother said the same to me.
(*Beaming*) But if no more you wish to eat,
Then p'rhaps a different kind of treat?
A sight to have you all agog.
Come. (*Indicating the swiss roll*) Seat yourselves upon this log,
And watch, as to a sweet refrain,
My little dancers entertain.

The children look at each other uncertainly, then move to the log and sit. Attrocia raises her stick and points L

There is a flash, music begins and several Gingerbread Men enter

Dance (*The Gingerbread Men*)

Hansel and Gretel watch in fascination as the Gingerbread Men dance. Attrocia stands behind the log. Toward the end of the dance, the dancers divide into two groups, move to opposite sides of the garden, and as the music ends, assume attitudes and freeze in position

(*Gloating*) And now if more delights you'd see,
We'll go inside. Admission's free. (*She indicates the door again*)
Hansel (*rising*) I don't think so. It's been a lovely dream but we'll be waking up soon so we'd better say goodbye. (*He walks* DR)
Gretel (*following*) And besides ... We don't really trust you. Why do you speak in *verse* all the time?
Attrocia (*forgetting her disguise*) Because, you nauseous little brat,
All witches have to speak like that. (*She realizes her mistake*)
Hansel
Gretel (*together*) Witches? (*They recoil from Attrocia*)
Hansel (*to Gretel*) Run for it.

Before they can move, Attrocia raises her stick, the Lights dim and the children freeze in their tracks

Attrocia (*gleefully*) Too late. Within my net they're caught.
And now a lesson they'll be taught.
Like all the rest, they're good as dead.
(*Triumphantly*) Transformed to sticky gingerbread ...

Cackling, she points her stick at the children. Nothing happens. In annoyance she tries again. Still nothing. She glares at her stick in disbelief

By the hairs on the tail of my old black cat,
My wand won't work. The battery's flat. (*She tosses the stick aside*)
(*Dismayed*) Or else — some dratted Fairy charm
Prevents my spell from doing harm?
(*Firmly*) No matter. Very soon she'll see
No fairy gets the best of me.
Another plot I'll quickly hatch.
To rid the world of all I catch.

With an evil cackle, Attrocia drags Hansel and Gretel into the cottage and the door closes. The Gingerbread Men quickly exit UL *and* UR

The Lights return to normal

Karl enters DR

Karl (*puzzled*) I don't understand it. I've done what the fairy told us and followed the path of primroses, but there's no sign of Hansel and Gretel or the other children. (*He sees the cottage and reacts*) What a strange little cottage. I thought I knew every inch of the forest, but I've never seen that before. (*He sees the notice-board*) And what's that? (*Reading*) "Do not press this button." (*Frowning*) How very odd. (*He moves towards the board*)

Audience response

Dickie dashes on R

Dickie Hiya, kids. (*To Karl; fiercely*) Gerroff me button, you barbarous brigand. (*He staggers about, gasping for breath*)
Karl (*turning to him, surprised*) Dickie. What are you doing here?
Dickie (*recovering*) Never mind what *I*'m doing. (*Accusingly*) What were *you* doing near me button board?
Karl (*taken aback*) I thought it was some kind of doorbell for the cottage over there. (*He indicates the cottage*)
Dickie (*turning to see the cottage*) Blimey. Where did that come from?
Karl I've no idea. But I'd like to know who it belongs to. And if Hansel and Gretel are inside. There's not a child on earth could resist something like that.
Dickie You're right. We'll knock on the door and ask, shall we? (*He moves to the door and makes to knock*)

Lucy hurries on R, *followed by the Dame in a fantastic new outfit*

Lucy *(anxiously)* Wait. Wait *(She hurries to Karl)*
Karl *(delightedly)* Lucy.
Dame *(gaping at the house)* Oh, I say …
Lucy *(breathlessly)* You mustn't go near that cottage. It belongs to a *witch.*

Dickie reacts and hastily moves away from the door

The missing children are trapped inside it and she's still looking for more. I heard her say so, myself.
Dickie *(alarmed)* What are we going to do?
Karl *(decisively)* Try to rescue them and hope the Fairy turns up in time to help us.
Dame *(glancing around, worriedly)* And where's Hansel and Gretel? Don't tell me *they*'ve been caught as well?
Karl I'm afraid it's possible. There's not a trace of them in the forest.
Dame *(horrified)* Oh, no.
Lucy *(quickly)* Don't worry, Dame Do-Good. If they *are* inside the cottage, Karl will save them.
Dickie Yes. And he won't be doing it by himself. *(Grimly)* If that rotten old witch is at home, she'll find she's got *two* of us to deal with.
Dame *(surprised)* You mean … you'll go in with him?
Dickie *(startled)* Me? *(He flounders)* I thought he'd take Lucy.

The Dame glowers at him

Karl *(soothingly)* There's no need for any of us to go in just yet. The first thing to do is make sure they're all still inside. So here's the plan. I'll keep her busy at the door while you go behind the cottage and look through the windows. If you do see the children, then that's the time we'll act.
Dickie *(blankly)* Aren't we acting now? *(Dismayed)* It's not just another rehearsal, is it?
Dame *(tiredly)* Oh, shut up and get back in your box. *(Concerned)* Oooh, I hope she's got venetian blinds round there.
Lucy *(puzzled)* Why?
Dame Well if she hasn't, it'll be curtains for all of us.

Dickie reacts, grabs the Dame and draws her quickly off, L

Lucy *(lingering)* You will be careful, won't you?
Karl *(reassuringly)* Of course. And when things are back to normal again, I'll make quite sure that nothing else has a chance to interfere with our wedding plans.
Lucy *(happily)* Then the sooner that happens, the better.

Song 15 (*Karl and Lucy*)

Sir Rupert (*off* R, *calling*) Help. Help.
Lucy (*startled*) That sounds like Sir Rupert. (*He glances around*) But where *is* he?
Karl (*looking off* R) He must be in the shed over there. We'd better find out what he's doing here and see what's wrong.

They hurry off R

(*Calling*) Hallo? Is that you, Sir Rupert? Is something the ——

There is a startled cry from both of them, and the sound of a slamming door

A moment later, Sir Rupert enters R, *smirking and holding a large key*

Sir Rupert (*triumphantly*) And that takes care of *them.* By the time they escape from that shed, I'll have rescued the brats myself and claimed the gypsies' reward. (*Smugly*) How lucky I followed young Lucy and Dame Do-Good to this edifice of excess eccentricity. Thanks to them, I'll soon be a hundred gold pieces richer — and owner of my very own cake and sweet shop. (*He chortles with glee*) Sir Rupert de Rottweiler triumphs again. (*He marches to the cottage door and knocks firmly. Calling*) Come out, you wizened old witch. I arrest you in the name of the law.

The Lights rapidly fade to Black-out

Scene 4

Behind the Gingerbread House

A lane scene, depicting a back view of the house in a half light

Dickie enters L, *followed by the Dame in another startling costume*

Dickie (*to the audience, softly*) Hiya, kids.

Audience response

The Dame reacts, then glances round nervously

Dame Oooh, I say. I don't like it here. It's all dark and gloomy.
Dickie (*airily*) Doesn't bother me. I'm used to being in the dark.

Dame (*acidly*) Yes. And you can say that again. (*Annoyed*) What do you mean, you're used to being in the dark? What dark do *you* go in?

Dickie (*defensively*) *Night-time* dark. When I go to *bed*. I can't get to sleep so I have to lie in the dark until it's morning.

Dame (*baffled*) Why don't you do what everybody else does and count sheep? By the time you get to a hundred, you'll be snoring like mad.

Dickie I know. But it wouldn't *work* for me.

Dame Why not?

Dickie I can only count up to ten.

Dame (*after a reaction; tiredly*) Go look through the window and see what the witch is doing.

Dickie (*glancing off* R *and recoiling*) Ooooooooh. She's coming towards it, holding a box of *crayons*.

Dame (*blankly*) What's she want crayons for?

Dickie So she can draw the curtains. (*He looks again*) Oh. She *has* done. We can't see anything, now. What are we going to do?

Dame (*thinking furiously*) We'll sneak in through the back door. (*Pointedly*) But don't let her see any footprints. Before we go in, make sure your feet are clean.

Dickie (*indignantly*) They *are* clean. It's me *shoes* that are muddy.

Potz and Panz enter, one L *and the other* R. *They are walking backwards in an exaggerated and cautious manner, totally unaware that they are not alone. The Dame and Dickie watch in fascination as the two men pass them and cannon into each other,* C. *Giving loud yells of fright, they turn and see each other, yell in fright again, then realize and relax*

Dame (*crossly*) What are *you* doing here? You're not supposed to be in this scene.

Potz (*plaintively*) We know. But we've just seen something horrible.

Panz nods vigorously, on the verge of tears

Dickie Oh, come on. French and Saunders (*or other duo*) aren't *that* bad.

Panz No, no. You don't understand. It's Sir Rupert. He was banging on the front door and shouting, and a nasty old witch came out and turned him into a gingerbread man.

Dame (*dismayed*) Ooooer.

Potz And now we can't find the way home.

Dickie (*scornfully*) Yes, you can. You go back the way you came. Follow the primrose path.

Panz But it's not there any more. That's why we're late. Sir Rupert told us to pick them all so he could sell 'em to the village flower shop.

Dame (*dismayed*) You mean we're all lost? In a forest full of ghosties and ghoulies? (*She glances around nervously*)

Dickie Don't worry, Dyspi. As soon as the Fairy arrives, she'll show us the way home. And anyway — there's no such thing as ghosties and ghoulies.

Potz Oh, yes, there is. Windsor Castle's full of 'em. My grandad got chased by 'em, once. All round the cellars, up the staircases, down the corridors, and finally — finally — they caught him by the ramparts.

Dame (*wincing*) Ooooooh. I bet *that* made his eyes water.

Panz (*airily*) Yes. Well they don't bother me, ghosts don't. I know how to frighten 'em off. I read it in one of them posh newspapers. You know. The one they print for super-intelligent readers. (*He looks smug*)

Dame (*impressed*) Oh, yes. The Mayor of (*local town*) gets that. (*She thinks*) Now what's it called? (*Remembering*) I know. The *Sun*.

Panz Anyway — according to a new scientific study, the one thing ghosts can't stand is live people singing. So if we all sang a little song, there isn't a ghost who'd dare come near us.

Everyone looks impressed

Dame In that case, we'd better sing something. And it might keep the witch away, as well.

Potz Good idea. So what are we going to sing?

Dickie How about, "She was only a constable's daughter, but she let the Chief Inspector"?

Dame No, no. We need something bright and cheerful. Let's sing *Supercalifragilisticexpialidocious*. We all know that one.

Panz Yes, but it's ever such a long word, isn't it? What if a ghost comes along before we've finished singing it?

Dickie We can do something that's never been done in any other pantomime for hundreds and hundreds of years. We'll get the audience to shout out and warn us. (*To the audience*) Will you do that, kids? If you see something creepy, just scream out as loud as you can, and we'll know it's around.

Audience response

Right, then. Off we go.

The quartet begin to sing

Song 16 (*Dame, Potz, Panz, Dickie*)

As they do so, a Ghost enters L, *flits behind them and exits* R

The audience reacts and the singers falter and halt

(*To the audience*) What's the matter?

Audience response

You've seen a *ghost?* .

The singers glance around quickly

Dame Well, *I* can't see anything.
Potz Me neither.
Dickie (*to the audience*) Where did it go?

Audience response

(*Indicating* R) Over there? (*To others*) It went over there.
Panz (*scornfully*) They're pulling our legs.
Dickie (*nervously*) We'd better have a look, just the same.

With exaggerated caution and glancing L *and* R, *they tip-toe* R, *then circle back to their original positions*

(*Relieved*) Well, there's nothing there now. I bet that song we were singing's frightened it off.
Dame (*brightening*) Oh, yes. So now we know it works, don't we?
Potz Let's sing another verse.

They begin to sing again

The Ghost enters R, *crosses behind them and exits* L

The audience responds. The quartet grinds to a halt again

Dickie (*to the audience*) What are you shouting for, now?

The audience replies, and the quartet appears scared

Is it still here?

Audience response

Where did it go this time?

The audience responds

(*Indicating* L) Over there? (*To the others*) It went that way. (*He indicates* L)

Dame (*nervously*) We'd better look over there, then.

They circle as before

Potz All clear on that side.

Dame We must have frightened it off again.

Panz (*proudly*) I said it'd work, didn't I? Let's sing some more.

They begin singing again

The Ghost enters L *and moves behind the singers to halt* C *and menace them*

The audience reacts. The singers stop

Dickie (*to the audience*) Has it come back again?

Audience response

(*Indicating* L) Did it go that way?

Audience response

(*Indicating* R) Did it go that way?

Audience response

Then which way did it go?

Audience response

Behind us?

Dickie, the Dame, Potz and Panz react in fear

(*To the others*) Listen. Listen. I'll tell you what we'll do. We'll count up to three, then turn round quick and grab it. All right?

They count. As they get to two, the Ghost bobs down; when they turn on three, they grab empty air. They turn to face the audience again and the ghost rises

Dame (*disgustedly*) There's nothing there at all. They're having marinations.

Potz Yes. *And* they're spoiling our song.

Panz (*scowling at the audience*) Go home, you rotten things. We're not going to listen to you any more. (*To the others*) Let's start singing again.

Dickie shrugs apologetically to the audience and the song begins again

The Ghost taps Panz on the shoulder. He turns his head, sees it, screams in fear and dashes off R, *followed by the Ghost*

The others stop singing

Dickie (*surprised*) What was that? Where's Panz gone?
Potz (*grimacing*) Must be that curry he had last night.
Dame (*sympathetically*) Vindaloo?
Potz (*nodding*) Six times today, already.

The trio begin singing again

The Ghost enters R *and taps Potz on the shoulder. Potz looks round, sees it, screams and dashes off, chased by the ghost*

The others stop singing

Dickie (*nervously*) Ooo-er. Now *he*'s gone as well.
Dame (*shrugging*) Well — we didn't really need him here, did we? Now we're on our own, we can sing by ourselves and get to know each other better.
Dickie (*startled*) Can we?
Dame Of course we can. We can put our cheeks next to each other, and you can put your arm round me — and if you're very very good — I might let you get a little bolder. (*She simpers at Dickie*)
Dickie Eh?
Dame Then *I'll* get a little bolder — and *you'll* get a little bolder — and *I'll* get a little bolder ...
Dickie We're not going to build a rockery, are we?
Dame (*disgustedly*) Oh, shurrup and sing.

They sing again

The Ghost enters and taps Dickie. He turns and sees it, reacts and dashes off, chased by the ghost

The Dame stops singing

(*Nervously*) Dickie? Dickie? (*To the audience*) Oh, I say. He's left me on me own. All by meself and nobody with me but me. (*Shrugging*) Oh, well. I don't mind singing on me own. I've got a big voice. Last time I sang on my own, half the people in the audience left to make room for it. (*Proudly*) I'm not called the Charlotte Church of Pumpernickel for nothing. (*She sings*)

The Ghost enters and taps the Dame on the shoulder. She turns to look at it. The Ghost screams loudly and exits L *in a panic. The Dame looks at the audience in bewilderment, then follows it off, still puzzled. The Fairy enters* R *in a white follow-spot*

Fairy At last … Attrocia's hiding place I've managed to locate,
And now she'll meet, I promise you, a very well-earned fate.
Her magic powers I'll take away. Her wits I'll dim and slow.
Her skills will shrivel on the vine, whilst other people's grow.
In short, she'll find to her dismay … and in this very hour …
It never … ever … pays to mock the Woodland Fairy's power.
(*She waves her wand*)

The Fairy exits R. *The follow-spot goes out*

Black-out

Scene 5

The Witch's Kitchen

A full set. This has a typical pantomime kitchen backdrop with window, shelves, etc., and various kitchen utensils hanging on the walls. Entrances L *and* R *are concealed by plastered interior walls which also are festooned with kitchenware; the witch's broomstick rests against the flat* DL. UR *is a huge oven with a large practical door. This is painted black and is set at an angle between the backdrop and the interior wall, thus affording an exit from the oven into the wings. Various large cooking pans are on top of the oven. Occupying the same position* UL, *but on a small brick plinth, is a large "cage" with a barred frontage. On the floor of the cage is a thin stick. A rough curtain can be pulled down to hide the bars and conceal what is inside.* C *of the room is a long counter for food preparation. In the* R *side surface of the work-top, a sizeable hole has been cut. Over this, a bottomless plastic washing-up bowl, painted to resemble pottery, is placed; inside this is a large ball of fresh dough. A large wooden spoon and a rolling pin are beside this, plus a chef's apron (or a pinafore) and an old tea-towel, the end of which drops below the front edge of the counter. A thick, rather battered, cookery book is* C *of the worktop; to the far* L *is a small stack of dinner plates (preferably unglazed ones, but if glazed, scored with a tile cutter). Under the counter is a bag of flour, a box of soap powder, a hand-brush and a small flower in a plant-pot*

When the scene begins, the Lights are on full. Hansel can be seen inside the cage, holding on to the bars; Gretel is scrubbing the kitchen floor with a brush DR, *with Attrocia watching her intently*

Hansel (*shouting*) Let me out of here. Let me out. (*He shakes the bars*)
Attrocia (*turning to him*) Alas, I fear, you beg in vain.
There's no escape from my domain
Now silence — or my wrath you'll feel.
I can't stand kids who shriek and squeal.
Gretel (*grabbing Attrocia's skirt*) Let him out, you horrible old witch.
Attrocia (*in mock shock*) Such temper. (*Snarling*) Nasty little brat.
You'll soon regret you called me that.
(*She pulls Gretel to her feet*)
Your tone of voice I'll swiftly change …
(*She suddenly releases Gretel and staggers against the counter, clutching at her head*)
What's happening? I feel quite strange.
My sight is blurred. My legs are weak.
My throat's so sore it hurts to speak.
My forehead's hot — my cheeks are, too.
(*She checks her pulse. Dismayed*) Oh, no. I must have caught the flu.
(*Weakly*) The room's a-spin. Perhaps it's best
To lie down on the bed and rest?
(*To Gretel, fiercely*) But don't think now, you've chance to flee
(*Indicating Hansel*) For *he's* still *there* and *here's* the key.
(*She pats her apron pocket*)

Attrocia totters off L

Gretel (*hurrying to the cage*) We've got to get away from here.
Hansel But how? (*Despairingly*) She says she's going to *eat* me.
Gretel (*reassuringly*) She doesn't *mean* it, Hansel. She's only saying it to frighten you.
Hansel Then why is she making me fatter? Every few minutes I have to drink another glass of her special mixture, and my clothes are bursting at the seams.

Gretel (*horrified*) Then you mustn't drink any more. If you stay thin, perhaps she'll change her mind?

Hansel (*sadly*) It's too late for that. Look at me now. (*He holds out his arms*)

Gretel You don't look different to me. And we know she's very short-sighted.

Hansel But she always squeezes my finger to see how much weight I've put on.

Gretel Then don't *let* her. Hold out that stick by your feet and let her squeeze that. She'll never know the difference.

Hansel (*brightening*) Oh, Gretel, you're the best sister I could ever have. Nothing frightens *you.*

Gretel It *does.* (*Firmly*) But I won't be scared of a rotten old witch. And besides — somebody out there's sure to be looking for us. Aunt Dyspi … Dickie Dymwit … Karl and Lucy …

Hansel Then all we have to do is hope they find us in time.

Song 17 (*Hansel and Gretel*)

At the end of the song, Attrocia enters L, *beaming*

Attrocia That little snooze has done me good.
Fresh colour's in my cheeks.
I dreamed the world was free of kids …
My nicest dream in weeks.
(*Briskly*) But now it's time to cook my meal.
Providing Hansel's fat. (*He moves to the cage*)
Put out your little finger, child,
And let me squeeze on that.

Hansel puts the stick between the bars and Attrocia feels at it without looking

(*Startled*) What's this? No fat? It's skin and bone.
He should, by now, weigh twenty stone.
(*Grimly*) But nonetheless I hereby vow
I'll dine upon him here and now.

Hansel and Gretel react as Attrocia hurries to the table and snatches up the cookery book

But first — I need to take a look
Inside my witch's cook'ry book. (*Finding a page and reading aloud*)
"To roast a child in pan or pot,
Make sure your oven's nice and hot."

(*Lowering the book and thinking*) Two-forty Celsius seems just right —
Or four-seven-five in Fahrenheit.
(*She replaces the book, moves to the oven, sets the dial, then moves to Gretel*) Now — whilst we wait for heat to build,
My water-bucket must be filled. (*She grabs Gretel's arm*)
So come with me, you scrawny lump.
I'll hold the pail and *you* can pump.

Hansel (*shouting helplessly*) Let go of her. Leave her alone.

Attrocia pulls down the curtain covering the cage front, then pushing Gretel in front of her, they both exit. As they vanish from sight, Dickie puts his head around the flat DR

Dickie (*brightly*) Hiya, kids. (*He comes on and glances round*) So this is IKEA.

The Dame hurries in DR, *dressed in another incredible creation*

Dame (*alarmed*) Keep your voice down. We're supposed to be full of surreptitiousness. Not shouting and bawling all over the place. What if there's somebody here? (*She glances round suspiciously*)

Dickie (*protesting*) But there isn't. There's nobody here at all. The Fairy must have turned up and got rid of the Witch while you were changing your frock, and the others'll be halfway home with the children by now. (*Put out*) And anyway — you've some need to talk about making a noise. You were yelling your head off in the garden.

Dame (*sheepishly*) Yes. Well I put my foot down a mole-hole. (*Glowering*) I hate moles, I do. They're always digging holes in the middle of somebody's lawn.

Dickie (*nodding*) They used to dig 'em in mine till I put a stop to it.

Dame How did you do that?

Dickie I took their spades away. (*He chortles*)

Dame (*ignoring him*) Well if everybody's been rescued, I'd better get back to the village and start doing the dinner. Hansel and Gretel'll be starving. (*She prepares to exit*)

Dickie Why not do it here, Dyspi? It's a lot bigger kitchen than yours so I can help you and we can carry it home on the witch's broomstick. (*He indicates it*)

Dame Oooh, good idea. (*Frowning*) But I'll tell you *one* thing that's always puzzled me. Why do witches go riding about on *broomsticks*?

Dickie (*scornfully*) Everybody knows that — (*to the audience*) don't they, kids? (*To the Dame*) It's 'cos you don't get long enough cables on vacuum cleaners.

Dame (*after a reaction*) Let's get on with the cooking.

They move behind the counter, Dame to the R *of the bowl and Dickie to the* L *of it. The Dame puts on the pinafore*

(*Briskly*) Now what do you think they'd like?

Dickie (*after a quick thought*) How about a sausage and egg pie?

Dame Oh, yes. They'd *love* that. (*Uncertainly*) Mind you — I've never made one before, so I'm not sure how to do it. I wonder if there's a recipe in this book? (*She picks up the book, opens it and reads*) Frog's eye pudding with slug sauce ... Earwig soup and crispy toadstools ... Baked centipede ...

Dickie Baked centipede? (*Grimacing*) Ugh. I bet that doesn't taste very nice.

Dame No. But at least we'd all get a leg. (*She pushes him playfully and chortles*) Oh, never mind a recipe. I'll make it up as I go along. (*She puts the book down*) We'll make the pastry first. (*She glances at the bowl*) No we won't — there's some here already. All we've got to do is roll it out. Get me a little flour.

Dickie ducks behind the counter and emerges with the flower in the plant-pot

Dickie (*proudly*) A little flower.

Dame (*rolling her eyes at his stupidity*) Not that kind of flower. (*Producing the bag of flour from beneath the counter*) This kind of flour. (*She vigorously shakes flour into the bowl*)

Dickie tosses the plant-pot into the wings, L, *then moves back behind the counter*

Dickie So what do we do next?

Dame We season it.

Dickie (*puzzled*) Eh?

Dame (*with emphasis*) Season it. (*She replaces the bag of flour under the counter*)

Dickie puts his head into the bowl and sneezes loudly. Flour is tossed into his face from below. He straightens up. The Dame turns back to him and reacts

Aaaaagh. (*Realizing*) I said season it, you fathead. Not sneeze in it. (*She lifts the dough from the bowl and looks at it disgustedly*) Look what you've done. (*She holds it out to him*)

Dickie (*peering at it*) What? What?

Dame You've covered it in germination. (*Seething*) Oooooh, it's a good job I've got my Kitchen Hygiene stercifficate and know how to put things right. (*She spits on the dough, rubs at it briskly with her sleeve, then slaps it down on the counter-top*) There. (*She smooths it with her hand*)

Dickie What do we do next?

Dame Well, *I'm* going to roll this pastry out, so *you'd* better find me some eggs.

Dickie (*brightly*) I'll look in the witch's hen-house.

Dickie exits DL

Dame (*calling after him*) And make sure they're *fresh* ones. (*To the audience*) Ooooh, I love baking. Especially if it's loaves of *bread.* There's not a woman in Pumpernickel makes a cottage loaf better than I do. And there's always a queue of fellers at me back door waiting to get their hands on my "bloomers". (*She picks up the rolling pin and begins to vigorously roll out the dough. As she rolls it away from her, it shoots off the counter-top and on to the floor. She puts the rolling pin down and dashes round to pick up the dough. Dismayed*) Oh, no. It's got dirt all over it. (*Grimly*) And I'm not surprised, looking at *this* floor. (*She slaps the pastry down on top of the counter, next to the tea-towel*) So *that* wants cleaning up before I do anything else. If there's one thing I can't *stand* it's a dirty kitchen. (*She gets to her knees in front of the counter, reaches up for the tea-towel but gets the pastry instead and without looking at it, polishes the floor furiously*) There. You can see the floorboards now. (*She notices the counter front*) But look at the muck on that. It must be a foot thick. (*Disapprovingly*) The way some folks *live.* (*She wipes it down with the pastry*) That's better. (*She looks at the pastry and reacts*) Ooo-er. I'd better clean it up before Dickie gets back. (*She jumps up, hurries behind the counter again, puts the dough on the counter-top and gets the box of soap powder which she sprinkles on to the dough. She then gets the hand-brush and brushes the dough briskly*) That's better. (*She puts the dough down and replaces the brush and soap powder box*) Now where is he with those eggs?

Dickie enters DL *with an open box of eggs. One of these is made of china, pottery or stone, one is "blown", and the remainder are fresh*

Dickie Here we are, Dyspi. One box of hen-fruit. (*He displays them*)

Dame Oooh, I say. Aren't *they* nice looking?

Dickie So what do we have to do with 'em? (*He puts the box on the counter*)

Dame Well first of all, we separate *two* of 'em.

Dickie (*eagerly*) *I* can do *that.* (*He takes two fresh eggs from the box*) I'll put one down here (*he puts it* R *of the counter*) and the other one here (*he puts it* L). There we are. Separated eggs.

Dame (*tiredly*) Not like that, you dopey drongo. They've got to be *beaten.*

Dickie Well, why didn't you *say* so? (*He gets the mallet from under the counter and flattens one of the eggs with it*)

Dame (*snatching the mallet from him*) Now look what you've done. You've *bruised* it.

Dickie (*puzzled*) Wasn't that right, then?

Dame (*irate*) Of course it wasn't right. Eggs are delicate. Eggs are fragile. Eggs are expensive. You don't bash 'em on the head with a mallet.

Dickie (*defensively*) I didn't bash it on the *head.*

Dame (*accusingly*) Yes you *did.* You hit it on the head like *this.* (*She flattens the second egg, then realizes*) Ooooh. (*She drops the mallet and glowers at Dickie*) *Now* look what you made me do. (*Grabbing the tea-towel and mopping up the mess*) Don't you know *anything* about eggs?

Dickie I know you can do *tricks* with 'em.

Dame (*baffled*) Tricks? With eggs?

Dickie Yes. I'll show you. (*He takes the "blown" egg out of the box*) One piece of hen-fruit (*he displays* it) and one plate. (*He takes a plate from the counter-top and moves* DL *in front of the counter*) Allez-oop. (*He tosses the egg into the air and catches it on the plate*) Taraaaaaa. (*He takes a bow and replaces the egg in the box*)

Dame (*impressed*) Oh, I say. I've never seen *that* done before. Can *I* have a go?

Dickie (*hastily*) Oh, I don't think you should, Dyspi. It's a man trick, that is. Girls can't do it.

Dame (*scornfully*) Don't be rickydoodelous. If *you* can do it, I'm sure *I* can. Watch this. (*She takes one of the fresh eggs, comes round in front of the counter and tosses it into the air*). Allez-ooops. (*She turns to pick up a plate, so missing the egg which falls to the floor and smashes. Dismayed*) Ooo-er.

Dickie You see? You see? I told you you couldn't do it. You've got to have 'em both in your hands *at once.* The egg *and* the plate.

Dame I'll try it again. (*She takes another fresh egg and a plate. This time she throws both into the air. Both fall to the ground and smash*)

Dickie No, no, no. You did it *wrong* again. You don't throw 'em *both.* You only throw *one.* Then you catch it with the *other.*

Dame (*light dawning*) Oh, I *see.* Throw *one* into the air and catch it with the *other.* (*Firmly*) Nothing to it. I'll have another go. (*She gets the china egg and another plate. This time she throws the plate into the air and holds out the egg to catch it. The plate misses the egg and falls to the floor to shatter*)

Dickie (*tiredly*) It's the *egg* you throw, not the *plate.* Try it again.

Dame (*taking another plate; grimly*) I'll do it this time if it kills me. (*She tosses the egg high into the air and holds the plate out to catch it. The egg shatters the plate and the pieces fall to the floor*)

Dickie (*frustrated*) That's *it*. That's *enough*. You can't do it again. There's only one egg left for the pie. (*He gets the broomstick and begins to clean up the mess*)

Dame (*protesting*) But I know how to do it, *now*. It's dead simple. I'll have one last try.

Dickie Well, you're not trying it with *this* egg. (*He throws the broom aside and snatches the egg from the box*)

Dame Yes, I am. *Give* it to me.

Dickie No.

Dame (*glowering*) Give me that *egg*.

Dickie No. (*Backing rapidly away from her*) You're not having it.

Dame (*advancing on him with menace*) If you don't give it to me, I'll tie a knot in your tongue and *swing* on it.

Dickie Come one step nearer and I'll *throw* it at you.

Dame (*scornfully*) You wouldn't dare. (*She rushes at him*)

Dickie throws the egg at the Dame. She ducks and it flies over her head and into the audience. Both look into the auditorium in horror

Dickie Sorry, missis (*or Mr*). It's a good job you're wearing yellow, isn't it?

Dame (*hastily*) I think we'll forget the eggs. We'll do a *sausage* pie instead.

Dickie (glancing off DR) There's some on the shelf over here.

Dickie exits DR *and re-emerges at once, holding a long string of pantomime sausages*

Here we are. (*He stretches them out*) Fresh made today from British *pork*, Californian *prunes* and hand-picked senna pods.

Dame *They* should keep us going for a while. But I'm not saying *where*. (*She picks up the knife*) Bring 'em over here and I'll cut them into ones.

The sausages shoot out of Dickie's hands and vanish into the wings with a whistle effect

Dickie (*gaping*) Blimey. They must have had baked beans in 'em as well.

Dame (*aghast*) Well, don't just *stand* there. Get after 'em.

Dickie dashes off and returns tugging on one end of a string of elasticated sausages which are firmly tethered off-stage

Dickie (*struggling to pull them onstage*) Quick, quick. They're getting away.

The Dame rushes DS *and grabs the waistband of Dickie's trousers*

Dame (*tugging fiercely*) Pull. Pull.
Dickie I *am* doing. They've wrapped themselves round the banister rail.

They pull harder

(*Straining*) Ooooh. Oooooh. They're off.

The Dame staggers backwards, Dickie's trousers suddenly ripping away in her hands, leaving him in a pair of garish boxer shorts. The Dame gapes at the trousers in dismay

Dame And so are *these.*

Dickie gives a shriek of horror as be realizes and scuttles off R, *followed by the Dame trying to give the trousers back. As they exit, Attrocia enters* DL. *She is followed by Gretel, who is struggling with a large pail*

Attrocia (*hissing*) Make haste. Make haste, you lazy girl.
For food my tummy aches.
(*She scuttles to the cage and throws back the cover to reveal Hansel again*)
You've peas to shell and roots to peel,
Whilst Hansel, in my oven, bakes.
(*In dreamy satisfaction*) With roasted chestnuts — and a glass
Of elderberry wine,
'Twill be the *perfect* meal on which
A witch like me should dine. (*She titters*)
Hansel (*afraid and shaking the bars again*) Let me out of here. Help. Help.
Gretel (*putting the pail down; calling*) Don't worry, Hansel. I won't let her hurt you.
Attrocia (*turning to her*) Stupid child. His fate is sealed.
You'll find I never bluff.
Now open up the oven door
And check the inside's *hot* enough.
(*She gets out the key and inserts it into the lock*)
Gretel But I *can't.* I mean … I've never *used* an oven before. And I don't know how to *do* that.
Attrocia (*fuming*) Oh, very well. I'll *show* you how
To work the old appliance.
There's nothing there to tax your brain.
It's hardly *rocket* science. (*She leaves the key and crosses to the oven*)
You twist the handle, just like this, (*she does so*)
And gently open wide — (*she opens it*)

Then test the heat by reaching out
To feel the air inside.

Gretel (*moving closer to Attrocia*) And do you only feel it at the *front* — or do you do it at the back as well?

Attrocia (*irritatedly*) All round. All round. You stupid Miss.
You feel all round. Like *this*. Like *this*.
(*She bends into the oven to demonstrate*)

Gretel rushes forward and pushes Attrocia

With a screech of fear, Attrocia falls head-first inside the oven

Gretel quickly shuts the door again, fastens it, then hurries to the cage and unlocks it. Hansel jumps out and they embrace

Karl and Lucy hurry on R *followed by the Dame in another bizarre costume. Potz, Panz, Gypsies and Villagers enter* L. *Karl is holding an axe, and the others a selection of rakes, pitchforks, swords, etc.*

Lucy (*seeing them*) You're safe.

The Dame hurries to them and hugs them

Gretel (*delightedly*) You found us. You found us. We thought we were lost forever.

Karl No fear of *that*. The Woodland Fairy told us where you *were*, but Sir Rupert locked us in the shed outside so *he* could claim the reward for finding the missing children. If this axe hadn't been in there, we'd probably *still* be trapped. (*He glances round*) But where are they?

Everyone looks round eagerly

Hansel (*sadly*) Out in the garden. Turned into gingerbread.

Lucy (*horrified*) Oh, no.

Everyone looks stricken

Karl And what about the witch?

Gretel Inside the oven.

All look at it

Hansel And if Gretel hadn't *pushed* her in there and shut the door, that's just where *I'd* have been.

The Dame hugs the children tighter

Gretel (*quickly*) But it wasn't my *own* idea. A little voice *told* me what to do. (*Puzzled*) Though I couldn't see *anyone* near me.
Lucy (*realizing*) The Forest Fairy. She *said* she'd made sure that nothing could hurt them. (*Firmly*) That witch got exactly what she *deserved.*
Karl (*downcast*) But too late to save the *other* children.

The Fairy enters R

Fairy Not so.

Everyone defers to her

I'll speedily erase
Of witch's spells, all earthly trace.
Each child to parent I'll restore
And nought shall harm them, ever more.
In short, once more this Sylvan scene,
Shall be as it has *always* been.

They all react with delight

Gretel (*hastily*) But what about the gold and jewels in the other room? Now the *witch* is dead, who will *they* belong to?

Everyone looks surprised

Fairy (*sternly*) Such treasure, you must understand,
Should rightly go to Fairyland.
(*Smiling*) But to mark your courage *and* your mettle …
Attrocia' s hoard is *yours*, young Gretel.

They all react with delight

Gretel Then I'll share it with *everyone* and Aunt Dyspepsia will never be poor again.

They all react with pleasure

Fairy So as this great adventure ends.
Be re-united with your friends.
(*She waves her wand*)

The missing children enter variously UL *and* UR *to be greeted by their parents*

Sir Rupert goes weakly to Potz and Panz

And ere to home you wend your way,
A cheerful song to end the day.

There is a cheer from everyone and they launch into a song of celebration

Song 18 (*Company*)

At the end of the song, there is general celebration

The Lights rapidly fade to Black-out

Scene 6

A Corridor in the Town Hall

A lane scene

The Lights are on full

Dickie enters R

Dickie Hiya, kids.

Audience response

Have you enjoyed yourselves?

Audience response

So have I. It's been a real adventure, hasn't it? We haven't had as much excitement since John Prescott (*or other unpopular politician*) had his helicopter crash. Yes. He got fed up of all the traffic jams, so he decided to learn how to *fly* one — and on his very first day he went up as high as a house. There he was — sat looking down at everybody — and he thought "I'd see a lot more if I went up a bit higher," so he pulled on his little joy-stick and up he went to *half a mile*. It was even better up there — he could see all over London — and it was lovely and warm. "Here," he thought, "it's good, this is. If I go up higher still, I can look over the fence at Tony

Blair's new house and see what they're up to". So he pulled on his little stick again and shot up to two miles high. (*He grimaces*) And *that's* when he had the accident. The sun went behind a cloud and it started to get a bit chilly — so he reached up and turned the overhead fan off.

Sir Rupert enters L, *followed by Potz and Panz*

Sir Rupert (*scowling*) Aha. Just the man I'm looking for. I know when the Fairy changed me back from being a gingerbread man, I agreed to let Lucy and Karl have their wedding here — but I'm not happy. Everyone but *me's* been given a share of the witch's treasure and I've been left with *nothing*.
Dickie Yes. Well it serves you right for being so nasty to everybody. (*To the audience*) Doesn't it, kids?
Sir Rupert (*glowering*) Well, I'm not *standing* for it. I deserve *something* as much as anyone else, so as Mayor of Pumpernickel, I'm going to claim that stupid button-board of yours and sell it to the highest bidder.
Dickie (*indignantly*) You can't do *that*.
Sir Rupert (*firmly*) Oh, yes, I can.
Potz
Panz } (*together*) Oh, no you can't.
Dickie
Sir Rupert Oh, yes I can.
Others (*with the audience*) Oh, no you can't.
Dickie (*giving in*) Oh, all right then. You can have it if you want. Besides — I don't know what'll happen if anyone *does* press the button.
Sir Rupert There's only one way to find out. (*He crosses to the* R *in front of Dickie*) Give it a press.
Dickie (*startled*) Me?
Sir Rupert Why not? It's your button. For the time being.
Dickie (*to the audience; nervously*) Do you think I should, kids?

Audience response

But — it might be a *bomb*.

Potz and Panz dash madly across the stage to join Sir Rupert. Dickie reluctantly approaches the button and timidly puts his finger out to press it. Changing his mind, he drops his hand and backs away. The others jeer at him. Annoyed, he gathers his courage, moves back to the button and presses it. There is a whirring as of clockwork, and a huge mallet comes out of the wings, R, *to strike Sir Rupert firmly on the head. His eyes cross and his knees buckle*

As Sir Rupert collapses, Potz and Panz grab him and drag him off R

(*Without looking*) No wonder they threw it away. It doesn't do *anything*. (*He turns to speak to the others*) Oh — they've all gone. Must be nearly time for the wedding. (*Remembering*) Ooooh — and that reminds me. I'm supposed to be out here looking for a *choir*. Well — they always have a choir at a wedding, don't they? And they never have enough *singers*. Have you heard 'em? (*He mouths silently with much face-pulling*) I mean, *that's* no good is it? You want 'em to bring the *roof* down. (*Realizing*) Here — I bet *you* lot'd be a *smashing* choir. I'll tell you what. I'll sing a little song, then you can all sing it after me, and we'll see if you're good enough for a wedding. Would you like that?

Audience response

Well, you're not going home till we've done it, so you'd better resign yourselves. (*Grinning*) One little song coming up.

The Song Sheet routine: Dickie sings the selected song, then the audience are encouraged to repeat it in the usual manner

Song 19 (*Dickie and audience*)

As the song is repeated for the last time, Dickie exits, waving, and the audience are left to finish on their own

The Lights rapidly fade to Black-out

Scene 7

The Mayor's Parlour and Finale

A splendid interior with a central staircase

When the scene begins, the lighting is full

The Villagers and Gypsies in resplendent costumes are dancing in partnership. At the end of the dance, half exit L, *and the other half*, R. *As they do so, the walk-down begins and proceeds in this order:*

Juniors
Villagers and Gypsies
Melindra and Roderigo
The Forest Fairy
Attrocia

Sir Rupert
Potz and Panz
Hansel and Gretel
Dame Do-Good
Dickie
Karl and Lucy

When the line-up is completed, the music stops

Lucy Our merry tale is over. All wrongs are put to right.
Karl We trust you've all enjoyed yourselves with us, this (*names day*) night.
Dame And if our time-loved jokes and songs have left you in fine fettle.
Dickie Your kind applause is our reward … so thank you from ——
Company *Hansel and Gretel.*

There is a reprise of one of the brightest songs from the show

CURTAIN

FURNITURE AND PROPERTY LIST

ACT I

Prologue

On stage: Hook on proscenium arch

Personal: **Fairy**: wand (carried throughout)
Attrocia: spectacles (carried thoughout)

Scene 1

Off stage: Small basket covered with cloth (**Lucy**)
Small plastic pail (**Hansel**)
Bag of coins (**Lucy**)

Personal: **Karl**: longbow and quiver of arrows, money pouch

Scene 2

Off stage: Notice-board (full description p. 14) (**Dickie**)

Scene 3

On stage: Brightly decorated stalls with goods on them
Balloons for **Balloon Seller**
Toffee-apples on a tray for **Toffee-apple Seller**
Ice-creams and ice-cream equipment for **Ice-cream Seller**

Personal: **Dame**: five pound note
Sir Rupert: four five pound notes
Dickie: five pound note

Scene 4

Personal: **Musical Director**: coin
Sir Rupert: coin

Scene 5

On stage: White picket fence
Giant lollipops
Huge chocolate Swiss roll
Fallen log

Off stage: Pail of blackberries (**Hansel**)
Lighted lanterns (**Mice**)

ACT II
Scene 1

No additional props

Scene 2

Off stage: Broomstick (**Attrocia**)

Scene 3

On stage: Avenue of giant lollipops
Shrubs with foil-wrapped sweets

Off stage: Gnarled walking stick (**Attrocia**)
Large key (**Sir Rupert**)

Scene 4

No additional props

Scene 5

On stage: Kitchenware on walls
Huge oven. *On it*: cooking pans
Cage with barred frontage and rough curtain. *In it*: thin stick
Long counter. *On it*: bottomless plastic washing-up bowl containing large ball of fresh dough; large wooden spoon; rolling-pin; chef's apron or pinafore; old tea-towel; thick, rather battered cookery book; small stack of dinner plates. *Under it*: bag of flour, box of soap powder, hand-brush, small flower in plant pot
Scrubbing brush for **Gretel**
Witch's broomstick against DL flat

Off stage: Open box of eggs — one china, pottery or stone, one blown, remainder fresh (**Dickie**)
Pantomime sausages (**Dickie**)
String of elasticated sausages (**Dickie**)
Large pail (**Gretel**)
Axe (**Karl**)
Rakes, pitchforks, swords (**Gypsies** and **Villagers**)

Personal: **Attrocia**: key in apron pocket

Scene 6

Off stage: Huge mallet (**Stage Management**)
Song sheet (**Stage Management**)

Scene 7

No additional props

LIGHTING PLOT

Practical fittings required: nil
Various interior and exterior settings

PROLOGUE

To open: Dappled lighting

Cue 1 **Forest Fairy** enters (Page 1)
White follow-spot on **Forest Fairy**

Cue 2 **Attrocia** the Witch enters (Page 1)
Green follow-spot on **Attrocia the Witch**

Cue 3 **Attrocia** exits L (Page 2)
Cut green follow-spot

Cue 4 **Fairy** exits R (Page 2)
Cut white follow-spot

ACT I, SCENE 1

Cue 5 Lane backdrop opens (Page 2)
Cross-fade from dappled effect to bright, sunny general exterior lighting

Cue 6 **Dickie** and the **Villagers** exit variously (Page 9)
Dim general lighting and bring up green follow-spot

Cue 7 The **Fairy** enters (Page 9)
Bring up white follow-spot

Cue 8 The **Fairy** exits (Page 10)
Cut white follow-spot

Cue 8 **Attrocia** exits L (Page 10)
Cut green follow-spot and return lights to bright sunny effect

Cue 9 **Song 4** ends (Page 13)
Fade to black-out

ACT I, SCENE 2

To open: Full general exterior lighting

Cue 10	**Attrocia** enters *Bring up green follow-spot*	(Page 16)
Cue 11	**Attrocia** exits *Cut green follow-spot*	(Page 16)
Cue 12	**Attrocia** enters *Bring up green follow-spot*	(Page 17)
Cue 13	**Attrocia** exits *Cut green follow-spot*	(Page 18)
Cue 14	End of **Song 5** *Fade rapidly to black-out*	(Page 18)

ACT I, SCENE 3

To open: General exterior lighting; warm and full

Cue 15	The **Fairy** enters *Bring up white follow-spot*	(Page 23)
Cue 16	The **Fairy** exits *Cut white follow-spot*	(Page 23)
Cue 17	**Song 7** ends *Black-out*	(Page 25)

ACT I, SCENE 4

To open: General exterior lighting; subdued

Cue 18	**Attrocia** enters *Bring up green follow-spot*	(Page 25)
Cue 19	**Attrocia** exits L *Cut green follow-spot and return to lighting state of the opening of* ACT I, SCENE 3	(Page 26)
Cue 20	**Sir Rupert** exits *Rapid black-out*	(Page 30)

ACT I, Scene 5

To open: General exterior lighting, diffused but not gloomy; fade as scene continues

Cue 21 **Hansel** falls asleep (Page 33)
Moonlight effect

Cue 22 The **Fairy** enters (Page 33)
Bring up white follow-spot

Cue 23 The **Fairy** exits (Page 34)
Cut white follow-spot

Cue 24 **Mice** enter with lanterns (Page 34)
Increase general lighting

Cue 25 Dance ends (Page 34)
Fade to black-out

Cue 26 Backdrop is flown (Page 34)
Bring up general exterior lighting; full daylight effect

ACT II, Scene 1

To open: General exterior lighting

Cue 27 The **Fairy** enters (Page 39)
Bring up white follow-spot

Cue 28 The **Fairy** exits (Page 39)
Cut white follow-spot

Cue 29 **Karl** exits (Page 40)
Rapid black-out

ACT II, Scene 2

To open: General exterior lighting

Cue 30 **Lucy**: " ... there'll be none left at all." (Page 42)
Begin slow fade of lights

Cue 31 **Lucy** exits (Page 42)
Dim lights more quickly

Cue 32 **Attrocia** enters (Page 42)
Bring up green follow-spot

Cue 33 **Attrocia** exits (Page 42)
Cut green follow-spot; return lighting to opening state

Cue 34 **Lucy** exits (Page 43)
Rapid black-out

ACT II, SCENE 3

To open: General exterior lighting; warm and full

Cue 35 **Attrocia** raises her stick (Page 45)
Lights dim

Cue 36 The cottage door closes (Page 46)
Lights return to normal

Cue 37 **Sir Rupert**: " … in the name of the law." (Page 48)
Rapid black-out

ACT II, SCENE 4

To open: General exterior lighting; half-light

Cue 38 The **Fairy** enters (Page 54)
Bring up white follow-spot

Cue 39 The **Fairy** exits (Page 54)
Cut follow-spot. Then black-out

ACT II, SCENE 5

To open: General interior lighting; full lighting

Cue 40 Song 18 finishes; general celebration (Page 65)
Rapid black-out

ACT II, SCENE 6

To open: General interior lighting; full lighting

Cue 41 **Dickie** exits; the audience finishes the song (Page 67)
Rapid black-out

ACT II, SCENE 7

To open: General interior lighting; full lighting

No cues

EFFECTS PLOT

ACT I

Cue 1	**Panz** mimes knocking *Very loud Westminster chime*	(Page 11)
Cue 2	The Lights come up to daylight *Cockerel crows loudly*	(Page 34)
Cue 3	**Hansel** and **Gretel** move US *Activate off-stage microphone for Attrocia*	(Page 34)

ACT II

Cue 4	**Hansel** reaches for a piece of the roof *Activate off-stage microphone for* **Attrocia**	(Page 43)
Cue 5	**Attrocia** points her stick L *Flash*	(Page 45)
Cue 6	Sausages shoot out of **Dickie**'s hands *Whistle*	(Page 61)
Cue 5	**Dickie** presses the button *Whirring of clockwork*	(Page 66)